EDGAR CAYCE RETURNS:

"None of the material that came from my voice when I was in trance...was my own thinking. It was that of one of my friends on the invisible side."

"Past life reading is a relatively rare gift. There are maybe twenty people in the United States who can really do it, although there are many more who say they can. I believe there are only four on the West Coast at the moment, in spite of the fact that it looks like thousands."

"The thing I find really distasteful right now, from my point of view, is that my personality and work are blown up almost to proportions of a saint."

"I suppose the reason why the aura has become so popular is that many people need to be able to pick up a book, run through a color scale, and make snap decisions about other people. The standard household variety of aura reader is so ridiculous that very few people would listen to them."

"There are those personalities (I'm sure you've run into them) who have very seriously misused what little psychic ability they had, and it was quickly removed. However, that didn't stop their careers as 'psychics'!"

—Edgar Cayce

THE COMPLETE
FROM HEAVEN TO EARTH
BY ROBERT R. LEICHTMAN, M.D.

The Psychic Perspective
The Inner Side of Life
The Hidden Side of Science
The Priests of God
The Dynamics of Creativity
The Destiny of America

FROM HEAVEN TO EARTH:

EDGAR CAYCE RETURNS

BY ROBERT R. LEICHTMAN, M.D.

ENTHEA PRESS
Atlanta, Georgia

ISBN 0-89804-839-7

TO CECIL GEORGE

PREFACE

Early in 1973 I began compiling a list of people who had made prominent contributions to the body of mankind's knowledge about its psychic and inner nature. My original intention was to write a collection of biographical sketches which would rekindle public interest in these pioneers of the human mind, and would add a needed perspective to the phenomena of inspired thought, creativity, and psychic ability. But as soon as I actually set pen to paper, the project began outgrowing my original intentions. For as I pondered the list of famous people I had selected—people such as William Shakespeare, Edgar Cayce, Carl Jung, Helena Blavatsky, Thomas Jefferson, and many others—I noted that all of them had left the physical plane. And then I was struck with a most singular thought: rather than just write biographies of these people, what if I could actually *interview* them!

Being familiar and comfortable with both the general nature of psychic phenomena and my own psychic abilities, this was an inspiration that seemed perfectly feasible as well as fascinating. And the possibilities were most enticing. I thought of the work of Edgar Cayce—his psychic readings on health, on reincarnation, and on the historical details of ancient civilizations. I wondered what he would have to say about his own work from his current perspective—thirty years after his death. I thought of Arthur

Ford, Eileen Garrett, and Stewart Edward White, all of them outstanding pioneers in the art of mediumship and the exploration of existence beyond death. Suppose they were given the chance to add to their immense contributions to psychic literature? Also on my list were people who had obviously led inspired lives but who had been less overtly psychic: Thomas Jefferson; Nikola Tesla, the electrical genius; William Shakespeare; Sir Oliver Lodge, a British physicist and early psychic investigator; and Sigmund Freud and Carl Jung, the developers of psychiatry. What insights could these gentlemen add to the inspirations and the efforts of their lifetimes? And then there were mysterious "occult" personages: Cheiro, the actor turned-palmist and numerologist who blazed a trail across the courts and drawing rooms of the rich and famous with his amazing predictions; the controversial Madame Blavatsky, founder of the Theosophical Society, who claimed to be in touch with superhuman "masters" in Tibet; and the clergyman turned clairvoyant and occultist, Bishop C.W. Leadbeater, who wrote voluminously about his own psychic investigations of life and human behavior. What was the real purpose of these remarkable people, and how were they able to perform the feats accredited to them?

What an opportunity it would be to talk with these great people and ask them about their own work! Surely, I felt, they all could add something new and vital to their life stories and their contributions—if just given the chance. Many myths and mysteries about them might well be answered. It would be possible, for example, to question Shakespeare about the riddle of the message on his tombstone. Or to ask Drs. Jung and Freud about their own psychic experiences—experiences that are barely mentioned in their writings and biographies. Did Jefferson really have the vision that history now attributes to him? Did Tesla really have the knowledge to harness the electrical power of Niagara and send it to Europe as easily as we now send short wave radio signals over thousands of miles? Was Madame Blavatsky actually in contact with great masterful intelligences who worked with Christ-like powers?

Eagerly, I began to anticipate the possibility of such geniuses commenting upon current conditions and trends in their respective fields. I wondered what Freud might have to say today about our modern sexual habits, about psychoanalysis—and about what Freudian psychiatrists have done with his work. How would Jefferson react to the problems and the size of twentieth century government? What would Sir Oliver Lodge have to say about modern psychic research?

But beyond all that, I wondered with natural human curiosity just what all these people are doing now. Are they continuing to follow the work they were engaged in during their lifetimes? Or are they pursuing new studies? In fact, do they even continue to be interested in what they accomplished during their lifetimes?

There was one other—perhaps personal—reason for interviewing the spirits of these departed greats, a reason that was most eloquently stated by H. P. Blavatsky during her life. In one of her letters to a student, she cast aside a personal inquiry to deliver an epistle about how the *real* Blavatsky was rarely visible even to her friends—not because she chose to hide it, but because such is the nature of the process of a soul incarnating into a physical body and personality. The portion of her being that remained in the "heaven world," she said, was the important part which directed the real work *through* the much more obvious part which people knew as her personality. If this were true of her, I reasoned, it must likewise be true of all of the other geniuses I had selected. Perhaps a psychic interview would provide a chance to talk with the *whole* person of each of these men and women for the first time—a chance to bring the whole person from heaven to earth.

Buoyed by my idea, I called a close friend, David Kendrick Johnson—an extremely competent and gifted medium. David has a special talent that makes it very easy for spirits to come through him—they find him compatible to work with. Indeed, because David is a first-rate artist in his own right, I knew that the group of geniuses I had chosen would find themselves "right at home" with his creative outlook on life. I also felt that if anyone would see the same potential for this project that I did, it would be he. And he did so—immediately, as though it were a familiar plan that had long ago received his agreement. We concluded that we should at least try it out. If we were successful, we would continue.

Both Dave and I are capable of direct clairaudient communication with "spooks"—a term of affection I have long used for referring to human beings who have left behind their physical bodies. Thus, we could have talked to the people on my list by this means. In fact, both of us have been quite friendly with a wide range of "spooks" for many years, and have come to highly value the friendship, camaraderie, and wise guidance of many such "dead" people. But instead of clairaudient communication, we decided it would be much more satisfactory for Dave to go into a mediumistic trance and allow the spirit of each person to speak through him, one at a time, while I conducted the interviews. So it was that we settled on the format that we have used in this series.

A few comments about the process of mediumship

should be made here. The patterns of speech in the interviews that will follow are all those of the medium. Thus, Dr. Freud does *not* speak with a thick Viennese accent—and it would be a mistake to assume that he should. The ideas of each spirit were translated into words by the medium's subconscious using his vocabulary and speech patterns; David's personality and voice box remained very much in evidence, even though they were being used and controlled by a different entity. This revelation may alarm some naïve people and draw protests from those conscious frauds who struggle so much to affect altered voices in the hope of mimicking mediumistic trances. But true mediumship seldom is accompanied by swooning or accents—unless the medium speaks that way normally.

Even though the ideas in these interviews are presented in David's words, the tone of each conversation is unique. A comparison between the interview with Madame Blavatsky and the interview with Sir Oliver Lodge, for example, will reveal that the tone of each is as different as those two fine people were different in their human personalities—even though they were contemporaries. And Bishop Leadbeater distinguished himself by experiencing more trouble coming through David than anyone else—he said it was the first time he had ever appeared through a medium. Thomas Jefferson, by contrast, heated David up—but immensely enjoyed the experience. And when Cheiro was interviewed, his natural charm and human glow were so noticeable that I shall never forget them.

In actual fact, talking to most of the people interviewed in this series was as natural as talking to old friends—and just as easy-going and enjoyable. They were greatly interested in being given the opportunity to express themselves once more. Just like any intelligent human who has something worth saying, they seemed to enjoy explaining their ideas and answering questions about their work. Nor had any of them lost his or her sense of humor in passing from the physical. Indeed, judging from some of the repartee in the interviews that follow, it's safe to conclude that there is wit after death. I have left in these lighter remarks in the hope that readers will be able to see that spooks are still very much human and still have brilliant minds. As Madame Blavatsky comments, "Why should we be sober all the time just because we are dead?" She also remarks that it is foolish for people to think that the dead all go away somewhere else and leave everyone on the physical plane to cope for themselves.

Thus, in editing the tapes of these conversations, I have left them nearly as they were in the original. I have removed a few personal references which would be of no interest to the reader and have improved the grammar and syntax here and there. But I have left the transcripts in an informal, conversational style—because that's the way it happened. And, when appropriate, I have added comments to describe the action or mood of the speaker. For instance, Madame Blavatsky—who was a chain smoker while alive—still drooled for cigarettes. So why not mention that she did smoke while using the body of Dave Johnson—who also smokes?

As we began this project, Dave and I quickly discovered that it had a life of its own. Indeed, our very first interview made it clear that even the basic idea for the set of interviews was not mine alone—but had been "suggested" to me by the spooks themselves. And they played a full role throughout. When one of them was "sitting" through David, most of the others were also there in the room, "eavesdropping" on what was said. This was commented upon several times, and quite often the person who was speaking at the moment would refer back to a point made by one of his colleagues several weeks before. I was also frequently aware that the spirits were communicating telepathically with me, even while they were speaking through David—psychically suggesting to me the next question I should ask! Indeed, Bishop Leadbeater clairaudiently dictated a whole list of questions to me the night before his interview began.

Then, once the interviews were completed, the spooks continued to prod us to finish the editing and writing, and to get the series published. They helped David in drawing the illustrations which accompany the text and often appeared to me while I was writing the short introductory sketches—to state the major points they wished me to make. And so, it would be quite fair to state that the project had a life of its own—quite apart from our own interests—just like the kicking of a growing fetus in the tummy of its mother. I hope some of this independent life will be apparent to the reader.

Undoubtedly some people may question the authenticity of these contacts with famous spirits. Cautious people will wonder if the whole effort isn't pure fraud. Others will decide that the presumption of such contact is outrageous. And yet, it is at least logical to make the attempt that we made. After all, who would know more about Edgar Cayce than Edgar himself? Who would know more about the actual relationship between Sigmund Freud and Carl Jung than these eminent doctors themselves? The potential of what can be accomplished through this kind of communication surely should be sufficient cause to *make the experiment*—no matter what one's previous conviction about survival beyond death might have been.

There is not sufficient space here to make a case proving the validity of psychic phenomena, mediumship, or survival of the personality after death. Nor is it necessary, for all of these matters have been *scientifically* proven many times over in other writings—indeed, in many of the books written by the people interviewed in this series. The doubting reader will find ample proof in the works of Sir Oliver Lodge, Stewart Edward White, Eileen Garrett, Madame Blavatsky, C.W. Leadbeater, Arthur Ford—and countless others. The interviews in *From Heaven to Earth* are offered in the hope that they are sensible and informative, rather than doctrinaire or categorical. It is hoped that the reader will take this material as food for thought and use it as part of his own inquiry into the mysteries of the "wonderful human mind," to quote Dr. Freud. The ideas presented are important enough to stand on their own, without being embroiled in a controversy about psychic phenomena, mediumship, or even whether we were able to contact the genuine spirits of these people.

The proper test of a good idea is its usefulness. The truthfulness and value of the ideas presented in this book will have to pass this test of usefulness by their successful application, not by mere claim, belief, or authority. Thus, let the reader measure the validity of these interviews—and the continued existence of these people—by the *value of what is said!* After all, these people were all great geniuses. A genius must act and talk like a genius and must say something significant, if we are to continue to accept him or her as a genius. And the spark of genius *is* abundantly manifest throughout this entire series.

We could have been far less controversial and avoided straining the credulity of potential readers by making this series a collection of academic discourses. But we hope the freshness of the approach we have chosen will contribute a touch of realism. After all, these people *are* alive and well and can speak quite eloquently for themselves, when given a cooperative mouth to use.

If these interviews in some small way serve to inspire a few to raise their sights and take a deeper look at the finer side of human nature, then our purpose will have been fulfilled. I might add that the purpose of the several spirits who graciously consented to be interviewed will also have been served. They, too, live and seek to be known and understood by those who have eyes to see and ears to hear.

—Robert R. Leichtman, M.D.

A NOTE FROM THE PUBLISHER

When the *From Heaven to Earth* series was first published twenty years ago, each interview was issued as a single book. There were twelve books in all, followed by a second set of twelve, making a grand total of twenty-four.

In 1990, Ariel Press decided it would be easier to keep all 24 interviews in print if they combined them into six books, each containing four of the conversations. So they did, reissuing the entire series.

The first book, *The Psychic Perspective*, contains interviews with Edgar Cayce, Eileen Garrett, Arthur Ford, and Stewart White. As might be expected, they talk primarily about the nature of mediumship and psychic phemomena.

The second volume, *The Inner Side of Life*, features interviews with C.W. Leadbeater, H.P. Blavatsky, Cheiro, and Carl Jung and Sigmund Freud. They talk about the inner dimensions of human psychology, the development of the mind, and the need for structure in our thinking.

The third book, *The Hidden Side of Science*, contains interviews with Nikola Tesla, Sir Oliver Lodge, and, from the second series of interviews, Albert Einstein and Luther Burbank. These great scientists discuss the materialism of modern day science and the need for science to explore the inner dimensions of life more effectively.

In the fourth book, *The Priests of God*, Dr. Leichtman interviews Albert Schweitzer, Paramahansa Yogananda, Andrew Carnegie, and Sir Winston Churchill. They discuss the role of intelligent service in the spiritual life.

The fifth book, *The Dynamics of Creativity*, features interviews with William Shakespeare and, from the second set, Mark Twain, Rembrandt, and Richard Wagner. They discuss the psychic and spiritual aspects of creativity in general and of writing, art, and music in specific.

The final book, *The Destiny of America*, focuses on the spiritual vision which led to the founding of America—and how well we are honoring this vision today. The first three interviews are with Benjamin Franklin, Thomas Jefferson, and Abraham Lincoln. The final interview is a "round table" conversation with seven significant spirits from America's past—Franklin and Jefferson, plus Alexander Hamilton, Harry Truman, Theodore Roosevelt, Franklin Delano Roosevelt, and George Washington.

This program has worked out well, except for two unexpected exceptions. The book-buying public continued to clamor for copies of *Edgar Cayce Returns* and *Nikola Tesla Returns* as individual interviews! In order to meet this demand, therefore, Enthea Press decided to reissue those two titles as separate books, even though they are also currently available in the full series.

Why did we feel this was necessary?

These interviews are unique. They elevate the art of mediumship to a practical, beneficial, and *intelligent* level. They set a new standard for all future mediumistic contact.

The spirits do not lay claim to any special knowledge unavailable to us on the physical plane. They avoid sermonizing and delivering stilted treatises. Instead, they chat with Dr. Leichtman in a free and easy way, often turning the tables on him by asking him questions that they want answers to. The type of intelligent sharing of ideas that results from this format is a rarity among mediumistic writings. Naturally, we want to make these books available to as many readers as possible—and introduce them to Dr. Leichtman, a truly remarkable individual.

Robert R. Leichtman is recognized as one of the best psychics in America today. Like Edgar Cayce, he has the ability to give detailed medical and psychological diagnoses of people he's never met—knowing only their names, ages, and where they live. Unlike Cayce, he does not have to go into a trance state to do this—he is able to work psychically while fully awake and alert. Born in Iowa, Dr. Leichtman received his medical education at the University of Iowa. He specialized in internal medicine, entering private practice in the Detroit area. In the late 1960's, however, Dr. Leichtman's interest in psychic and spiritual growth caused him to close his practice and devote his energies to personal psychic work, lecturing, writing, and teaching the principles of esoteric psychology.

The majority of his professional psychic work is as a consultant for psychiatrists, psychologists, and medical doctors throughout the country. His teaching is aimed at helping people understand their lives and develop their own psychic abilities and creativity. Dr. Leichtman is also a co-author of *Active Meditation, Forces of the Zodiac, The Art of Living* and *The Life of Spirit* essay series published by Ariel Press. He currently resides in Baltimore, where part of his time is spent working at the healing services of the New Life Clinic. He has just issued a new book, *Fear No Evil.*

Through Dr. Leichtman's effort, the spirits interviewed have been given the opportunity to return from heaven to earth. And they have given the rest of us a marvelous glimpse into the workings of genius—and the nature of the world of intelligence beyond physical life.

—Carl Japikse, 1998

THE FIRST INTERVIEW

Many of the greatest advances in civilization are the products of a single inspired human being who has reached his or her proper time and place in the course of history. A single Nikola Tesla or Sigmund Freud can revolutionize science and technology or remold society with his insights and labors. As a group, such geniuses stand on the frontiers of human knowledge and boldly gaze into territory previously unexplored by humanity—indeed, unknown to it. Their voices are never silenced; they live on in every by-product of their work. An echo of Dr. Freud is heard in every psychiatrist's office and in every class in psychology. The spark of insight of Nikola Tesla glows once again every time we flip on a light switch or otherwise benefit from the long-distance transmission of electricity. There are many, many others as well whose works have been embraced and absorbed by humanity and its culture.

And yet, we need not be content with just an echo of such genius: the voices of these pioneers can and should be *literally* heard anew. Their minds still live on even though their bodies do not, and they continue to involve themselves in work that parallels the efforts of their physical lifetimes. They can be contacted; they can speak again! And when given that opportunity by those who live now in physical bodies, these minds can continue their work on the physical plane by adding new insights and by stimulating the minds of people active in their respective fields today.

The choice of the people interviewed in this series is heavily weighted toward those who were gifted with unusual inspiration and vision. Their genius, in most cases, seemed to be fed from some intelligence or intelligences beyond the physical plane. And their minds seemed to have the capacity to be attuned to a hidden realm where they found the insights and the understanding which made possible their important contributions. How their genius and their minds worked deserves a great deal of attention. But it's even more important to learn how we, too, can think in the same modes of genius: to behold their insights for ourselves and to participate in the same creative processes. Thus, it's both natural and proper to investigate their examples, so that we may discern how to expand our own minds and reach their heights.

In talking with such people, it becomes apparent that there is a very real and powerful coordinating intelligence that oversees the evolution of humanity and civilization. That such guidance exists should inspire and reassure all of us. We must learn that no one of us ever stands alone, no matter what our questions or problems. Assistance is available—if we only understand that cooperation with this overshadowing intelligence is possible.

As I started this series of interviews, I began to realize that there was one spirit entity in particular who was coordinating the project on the inner planes, just as I was coordinating it on the physical. To make sure that we had all of our signals in agreement, I decided to consult briefly with this person. As will be obvious, I did not know who this person was by name—nor did I know a number of other details related to the project. I have decided to include this short interview here, so that the reader can learn about the format we decided on in the same way that I did.

In this first interview, David Kendrick Johnson is the medium and I am the interviewer. The first voice belongs to Rosie, who is one of David's closest friends in the spirit. Technically, she is known as a spirit guide or control. Rosie, who is also called "Wildrose" and "Rosebud," is a very feminine lady with an impish sense of humor. Yet she also is a powerful person who tolerates no nonsense, in spite of her girlish wit. Ordinarily, she "warms up" the medium prior to the appearance of the main spirit to be interviewed. She also serves as a "mistress of ceremonies" for the proceedings. Although her appearance at the start of this session is very brief, she will pop in frequently throughout the whole series—and also be referred to often by the spirits.

Rosie: I'm curious about whom you want to talk to.

Leichtman: Well, I suppose whomever is in charge of this project. I'm not really sure who that is.

[There followed a pause while Rosie left and was replaced by another spirit.]

New voice: Do you suppose that if I announce myself by name that I will get a plug in your book? You are not even intending to write about me, because you've probably never heard of me.

Leichtman: Oh, I will certainly dedicate the book to whomever really is the inspiration for it.

Voice: Well, I'm an English disciple of the being that you know of as D.K. [Djwhal Khul, one of the Tibetan Masters prominent in the writings of Helena Blavatsky, Alice Bailey, and others]. It is now my turn to assist with a piece of writing that is a part of the series of writings that was begun a number of years ago, as you have already suspected. I am in a state where I am sometimes in the flesh and sometimes not.

Leichtman: Do you mean that you are now incarnate?

Voice: Some of the time. I am at the moment, of course.

Leichtman: What were these previous writings that this project will be associated with?

Voice: The writings that introduced to the western world the teachings of the Tibetans, beginning with the works of Madame Blavatsky. And there were others.

Leichtman: Who were the others?

Voice: Many, many people whose writings have not come to the fore, plus the ones that you know—Mrs. Bailey, Mrs. Besant, and so on. And there was quite a bit of work done with Charles Leadbeater. He was a very easy channel. You see, I was there when the being you know of as D.K. was working with these people. Leadbeater was easy to contact—the easiest of the group, really. He could receive us in his ordinary state of waking consciousness. Mrs. Bailey had to alter her state somewhat.

As a matter of fact, I was one of the "Edgar Cayce voices," but not nearly so prominent as the being known as Michael. So you see, your impression that the whole project has continuity is very apt. There is a historical purpose for all of this, although it may not be apparent to you.

Incidentally, I can give you a name to call me, although it's a *nom de guerre*. We shall have to use "Cecil George." I was a titled Englishman who was born and brought up in northern China. I *would* have been titled, I should say. But one of my tutors in China was involved in the Tibetan teachings of the Ancient Wisdom, and I ran away from home at the age of twelve to join in this work. I felt more at home with the Orientals than the English. As a matter of fact, I never left Tibet after that.

All of the people that you wish to include in this project are quite eager to cooperate. Only one, Count Hamon [Cheiro], is now incarnate. He will be fairly easy to contact, but it will have to be tried some time late in the evening. I suggest you plan ahead for it. And have the sitter [the medium] get a little tight. Sometimes it's easier to get him completely out of the way if he's a bit tight. He also enjoys it.

[Laughter.]

Leichtman: Are we correct in assuming that these interviews should be conducted through David in full trance? Or is it better for one of us to converse with these people in

CECIL GEORGE

a semi-conscious psychic state using our clairaudient abilities?

Cecil George: Use the trance. You might even include an edited portion of the conversation we are having now, as part of the prologue. I may have some more things to say later; it depends on how things go.

Leichtman: I have a list of twelve people to be interviewed. Are these names satisfactory?

Cecil George: Oh, yes. In a sequel we are planning to include Darby and Joan, because they wish to contribute, too. But this is not the time for that. [Darby and Joan were friends of Stewart Edward and Betty White who helped bring through the materials for the book, *The Unobstructed Universe*. Apparently Joan couldn't wait for a sequel; she appeared briefly in the conversation with Stewart Edward White.]

Let's see. You are including Shakespeare. Rembrandt would like to participate in the sequel. It would be good to include an astrologer then, too, but it would have to be one of great stature. We are also hoping that later you can interview some of the more popular psychic figures, such as Dion Fortune.

Leichtman: The ones I chose are those that I thought would provide a balanced spectrum, so that not everyone is a psychic "reader" or fortune teller. Arthur Ford is a very good man and did many wonderful things, but his type of psychic endeavor is stressed too much. A discussion of psychic work needs to focus on the type of psychic who exhibits genius—the kind of person who is creative or who has remarkable insight into the nature of life. Some of the ones I've chosen are not household names, so to speak, but they are all famous in their own right.

Cecil George: Yes. If you want a modern American

medium, pick Edgar Cayce, because he is so well known to the American public. I believe he has some remarks to make that would be shocking to the right people.

Leichtman: Very good. Obviously, I've left out many people. In the realm of creativity, I have chosen William Shakespeare and an inventor, Nikola Tesla. I almost picked Edison, but I decided that Tesla would be a better example for our purpose.

Cecil George: Oh, yes. David has a great curiosity about this man. Having recently done a reading that touched on Tesla, he has a great interest in him. The remarks that you have made about Tesla have also intrigued David. Could you get him something to read about this man?

Leichtman: Yes, I will. And I hope that Tesla comes through with a little touch of wit. There is a quotation attributed to him that I use in my lectures; I'm not sure, but it may be apocryphal. It's about people spending the first half of their lives learning all about the things they can't do—and the last half of their lives not doing them. *[Laughter.]*

Cecil George: He did not say it in so many words; it was more a very apparent attitude that he had.

Leichtman: To go on about the outline of the book, I would like it to state something about the nature of the psychic process—that it is something more than just fortune telling. It includes genius and creativity.

Cecil George: That will come out in the body of the interviews, I believe. But it will be necessary to stress that the power to be psychic *is a power*, and is not by itself a spiritualizing agency.

Leichtman: Yes, that is usually not emphasized enough. The spiritual elements in all of this work are not the visions and the voices or the mediumship, but rather the pursuit and attainment of an expanded awareness and an understanding of ourselves and our lives. These are the spiritualizing elements.

It's too bad that more people don't realize that awareness is a talent that we can acquire with specific training. It isn't something that we have to be born with at all. There are steps that we can take to develop it—at least to achieve self awareness and self understanding. Psychic awareness is a capacity that can be consciously strengthened and expanded by deliberate intent. While it isn't quite the next best thing to sainthood, it is a bit more complicated than just learning how to play golf. And it can be of enormous practical value.

Cecil George: Yes. You might say that we have used our psychic ability to the point of sainthood when we can cross the Sea of Galilee without getting our toes wet. *[Laughter.]*

Leichtman: Very good! Now, one more point about the organization of the project. I intend to do a very brief biographical sketch about each of these people. It should be reasonably brief, right?

Cecil George: Say what you need to say; let the length take care of itself. If you keep your biographical comments simple and readable and hit the important points, it will be best.

I want to say this gently, as I don't wish to sound as though I'm being critical. You have a fine mind, but sometimes you write in a type of "intellectualese" that would be beyond most readers.

Leichtman: I think I can take care of that. I want to include in the biographies just enough material to acquaint the readers with the general work of the spook being interviewed.

Cecil George: Let me suggest this: you were talking

with David earlier today about the "genuine Madame Blavatsky." I would encourage you to include that sort of remark in the biographies—remarks that are based on the insights you have into the significance of these people, from the reading you have done. And as you have said, you definitely need to point up the contributions that these people have made. There should also be comments about the character or nature of these people now—such as commenting that Madame Blavatsky comes through as being sweet and refined. She can come across this way because Lumpy [Mr. Johnson] is a refined young man, too.

Leichtman: Of course, she really *is* gentle and refined.

Cecil George: On the inner planes, David has contacts that do not allow someone to come close to him who would not be gentle.

Leichtman: I understand.

Cecil George: And you might also make some remarks to the effect that I don't speak with an English accent. I don't even necessarily speak with my native vocabulary, because I must use the instrument available to me—or something like that. You know how to put it.

Leichtman: Yes: you impress your ideas rather than your verbalized words on David's subconscious. Therefore, the voice and style of speaking are still David's.

Now, when these people do come in to speak, how do they want to do it? Do they just want to speak by themselves, or—

Cecil George: For the purpose of this project, it would be good for you to act as an interviewer, just as you are doing now—to keep the conversation going. It would also make it a bit more interesting reading.

Leichtman: Perhaps in the format of the interviews done in news magazines?

Cecil George: Yes. And it would also be good to introduce the book with some comments about Lumpy and his work. Make it a personal statement. You don't need to push him in any sense, but it would be good to introduce him to the readers.

Well, it's a distinct pleasure to talk to you with my own thoughts. I know the rest are very much looking forward to this particular project. We are hoping you can have it pretty much completed in a few months—at least to the point where you can start revising.

Leichtman: Yes. I'll have to move quickly to get the background reading done, but it will be possible to work that fast.

Cecil George: The evening with Shakespeare is going to be very interesting. In some of these sessions you should feel quite free to invite other people to sit in and add their questions and comments.

Leichtman: Yes, especially those who have a particular fascination with and knowledge of that person and his work. I am hoping, by the way, that we can promote the book with a tour of TV interviews or lectures.

Cecil George: As a matter of fact, we hope that eventually you and Lumpy will be something of regulars on television, primarily holding mediumistic interviews just as we are conducting this one. A television station is ordinarily a difficult place to do a trance, but David seems to be able to manage it.

Leichtman: Perhaps later we can interview Rembrandt—maybe even Leonardo da Vinci.

Cecil George: You could include Leonardo if you wish, but Rembrandt might be a better choice. Rembrandt was perhaps the more human—that is, someone who was expressing his humanity through his psychic ability.

Leichtman: Very good. We will need a musician sometime, too.

Cecil George: And I believe there is something that needs to be contributed by Talbot Mundy in one of these books. It relates to the real structure of world government.

Leichtman: Do you mean something that parallels his book, *The Nine Unknown?*

Cecil George: Yes. Of course, there are more than nine.

Leichtman: Well, it all sounds very exciting.

Cecil George: It has been a pleasure talking with you about it. Unless you have some additional questions, I think we are about finished.

Leichtman: I'm quite satisfied with what we've covered.

Cecil George: Then I shall bid you good afternoon.

Subsequent to this interview, David and I held additional sessions in which the persons selected as subjects appeared briefly to talk about the topics they wished to discuss. I will include a few extracts for each individual here, collected from several trance sessions:

Edgar Cayce: I would like to talk about the broad scope of my work and how it was intended to be continued after my passing from the physical plane. As you know, I was a medium who worked with a large number of entities on this side, where I am now. In fact, I would like to bring along Michael, who was one of the main spirits who worked with me. He actually did many of the readings. Michael was especially interested in the health readings, as he used to be an herbalist doctor at one time in the distant past.

I would also like to talk about the need to develop an

organization where psychics could be trained and work. This was something which I had hoped would have been accomplished in my lifetime, or as a result of my life work. I should add here that my interest in the psychic work and readings is still quite strong. I have not gone away somewhere where I cannot be contacted. In fact, there are many of us who worked on the readings who are still quite available for the type of mind who is capable of cooperating with us.

William Shakespeare: I will talk on English letters, grammar, and creativity. I would also like to invite the Japanese dramatist Monzaemon Chikamatsu to join me, as we did the same thing at the same time. He was the "Japanese Shakespeare." Of course, in Japan I am known as the "English Chikamatsu." I also would like to talk about aspects of the Elizabethan period that are important to modern times. And I should mention that I wrote *all* of my own plays.

However, I did write *Julius Caeser* and *A Midsummer Night's Dream* for a marionette theater.

Cheiro (Count Hamon): I wish to talk about mantic devices—the Tarot, astrology, the I Ching, and so on—and how they are used for divination. It's not necessary to be psychic to work these devices, but it does help. I will stress the need for responsible, quality work in reporting prophecies and giving psychic advice, and the importance of intellectual study in preparing to be a good psychic or mantist. The style with which a psychic works is also a matter that we should discuss. It must be based on intelligence and discernment—which are often lacking today. And I would like to correct some of the notions concerning my work that have arisen since my lifetime.

Presently, I am incarnate as a three-year-old child, so

I can be available for these sessions only while my physical body is asleep. The hours for these sessions should be rather late and broken into three parts. As you know, it is possible to appear as a spirit at a seance even while you are incarnate in a physical body.

As you might surmise, there will be a sudden recurrence of my work in the world a few years from now.

Dr. Carl Jung: I would like to invite Dr. Freud to come along with me for this interview. We both have a number of things to say about the development of psychiatry in our time, as well as the use of this original work now. We would also like to discuss the vast influence of psychic (or what I would term "para-psychic") events on the human mind, whether it is neurotic or healthy. Dr. Freud and I both had a number of para-psychic experiences during our careers. We would like to discuss some of them, as it is now time to bring them out in the open. The operation of the human mind is a process that cannot be completely understood unless these psychic energies are looked into more seriously—and comprehended.

Charles W. Leadbeater: I wish to talk about what really happens during hypnosis and during the use of some of the newer techniques in psychology. Some of the phenomena that transpire are invisible except to the clairvoyant or someone with my perspective. If the actual effects of certain techniques were known, I believe that many of these techniques would be abandoned rather quickly. I also wish to talk at length on the effects of drugs on the mind and the emotions—especially psychedelic drugs.

Sir Oliver Lodge: I will be talking on the difficulty of the early work in Spiritualism. The attempt to do definitive research was much more frustrating than it is today. And I will have a few comments to make on the present state of psychic research. Raymond, whom you know as my son from that lifetime and the subject of my book on survival after death, will also come along to add his comments.

Thomas Jefferson: I plan to comment on the original intent and purpose of the Founding Fathers, in our effort to set up a foundation for a spiritualized government. I also want to speak about the American Spirit.

Arthur Ford: I am trying to decide what to do. The main point I wish to make clear is the true role of the psychic in the church. I hope to give some historical perspective to this topic, as well as comment on the future of the psychic in the church. I would like to see a return to the simplicity of the church before the Catholic Church was organized. Christianity came into a world full of stables of psychics, seers, and so forth. There was the same range of psychics as there is now: from the very few with excellent talent down to the phony "Madame Zenobia" fortune-teller type. The Christian church had to compete to exist; thus, for many years it did develop psychics within the church, but not in the way that the Spiritualist Churches are doing it now. The Spiritualists have lost sight of Christianity a bit. It's gotten to the point where there are Christian and non-Christian Spiritualists.

I received teachings from the invisible world that I never talked about, and I would like to mention them in my interview. I would also like to talk about the "Mr. Sun Moon" who is mentioned in my second book. In the light of the turn of events, I think that what I said about him needs some clarification.

I expect that Fletcher [Arthur's chief spirit control while he was alive] will also step in to give a few extra comments on psychic matters and mediumship, and what he actually did in working with me.

Helena P. Blavatsky: I would like to talk about the shortcomings of American culture—in particular, the gross lack of attention given to maturing the mind. I want to emphasize that people must learn to stimulate and train their minds and their thinking, whether they want to be a good scientist, a good psychic, or even a good mother and housewife. I also will have a few words to say on hypnosis. As you know, I was rather severe in my comments about the use of hypnosis during my recent career, and I wish to emphasize its dangers again.

Nikola Tesla: I wish to comment on the lack of understanding and use of inspiration on the part of modern science and scientists, as well as their disregard of the actual physical phenomena about them. And I would like to say something about the direction that science must take in the future.

Eileen Garrett: I will talk at length on the mechanics of the medium's trance. I have only been "over here" for a short while, and it will be a bit disconcerting for me to "be" a man again—at least for the length of the trance while I am using the medium's body.

Stewart Edward White: I believe that Betty or Joan will have something to say about preparing yourself to be psychic if you should happen to discover that you have some unfolding psychic abilities. Along with this, one of us will have some comments about the "rape of the mind," plus a few more things to say about existence on the other side of things—what we called "the unobstructed universe" in our books. As you know, every human being also has an existence in the so-called invisible realms or inner planes. This existence is simultaneous with the physical one. This is a fact that people can no longer afford to ignore, as it is the key to understanding themselves and the world around them.

❧ ❧ ❧

In the interviews that follow in this series, many bold statements are made. For instance, Sir Oliver Lodge takes psychic researchers to task rather harshly. Edgar Cayce expresses displeasure with what has been done to his work by those who now regulate it. Others were outspoken in their criticism of the lack of discernment and responsibility on the part of their own colleagues in their respective fields. These comments have been left intact, even though they may shock a few. It is not our purpose to needlessly offend anyone; however, to properly honor the spirits, we have left these sections unedited. If there is any merit in the charges, then history will have to be the judge.

Many times we have been cautioned by the spirits to allow people to decide for themselves the value of an idea, but to never apologize for the truth as we are able to see it. It is with this intent that the record of these conversations is offered to the public.

EDGAR CAYCE RETURNS

Almost everyone in America who has heard about psychic phenomena knows who Edgar Cayce was. Millions have read the scores of books that have been written about him and his work; even more have heard about the prophecies he made, the health advice he gave, and the information that he reported about ancient civilizations. Probably more than anyone else, Cayce made it possible for vast numbers of modern skeptics and doubters to approach the subject of psychic perception and accept its validity. The quality of his work and the style in which he did it distinguish him as a worthy model for all psychics to be guided by.

Cayce's work is the greatest popular source of psychically-derived information in the United States. He left behind him thousands of personal psychic readings, all of which have been preserved and catalogued, so that they may be used in research. Nearly every day during most of the first half of the twentieth century, Cayce would quietly lie down, loosen his collar, and slip into a deep trance. Then, after a few moments, his voice would announce that he was ready for whatever questions were to be answered. What followed sometimes was a detailed description of the illness of some person many miles distant and totally unknown to Edgar. Or it might be a thorough record of several past lives of the individual who requested the reading. At other times psychology, religion, philosophy, or even the nature of psychic phenomena would be discussed. His voice gave fascinating information about the life of Jesus, Atlantis, the origin of mankind, and the nature of man's inherent divinity and what must be done to honor it. At the end of a session, the suggestion would be given to awake, and after another few moments, Edgar would sit up, rubbing his eyes. He never seemed to recall anything that his voice had said during the trance. Often, he was startled by the profundity of the comments he had made in this fashion. Alien philosophical concepts, foreign words, and totally unknown facts were recorded coming from his mouth.

At first, these trance states were a great mystery to Edgar, but in time he grew to accept both his unusual ability and much of the content of what he said. Of course, what Cayce was doing when he went into trance was a form of mediumship. He withdrew his consciousness from his physical body while a spirit entity—someone who has passed beyond the physical plane, yet remains alive and aware—temporarily assumed control of the voicebox of his physical body. It was Edgar's many spirit friends who actually "authored" the messages that came through his mouth. Through this odd sort of partnership between heaven and earth, a tremendous amount of important and provocative information was communicated for our use. Today, human understanding is much richer as a result. Perhaps most remarkable of all, anyone who can read has access to this great treasure. The record of Edgar's work is now so well published that one can hardly visit a local supermarket or drug store without being able to purchase several paperbacks about it.

The one drawback to Cayce's popularity today is that the fame of his work has attracted many people who are more interested in basking in the glamour and glitter often associated with psychic phenomena than in seriously pursuing their own development as purposeful, mature human beings. This cult of Cayce worshippers has virtually elevated Edgar to the status of a saint. They try to keep secret the fact that Cayce worked as a medium, apparently believing for some reason that the word "medium" would cheapen his contributions to mankind. They attempt to place him in a special category unattainable to the rest of us.

Such sentimentality and fanaticism destroy intellectual integrity. It is inaccurate and unintelligent not to recognize the obvious facts in any situation. To state that Edgar was a medium, that the messages which came through him were the thoughts and ideas of a variety of spirit entities, in no way detracts from the value and the quality of the contribution Cayce made. The thoughts and ideas have merit and importance by themselves. It is not necessary to create a myth to encase and protect them. Myths only obscure the importance of Cayce's work; the facts reveal its true value.

I am one of Edgar Cayce's greatest fans. A large share of my introduction to real psychic work came from studying his biography and material taken from his readings. To me, he is a great model for the sensible role that psychic and mediumistic work should play in our culture—a model of how psychics should apply their talents and also a model of how the general public should interact with psychics. Perhaps more importantly, he is also a marvelous inspiration for the proper way that psychic research should be conducted.

When I first read his life story, I was able to identify with his struggle to accept his own ability, his disappointment with the skeptics about him, and the awful treatment that he received at the hands of the scientists of his day. I grieved with him as he coped with the concept of reincarnation, while trying to maintain his faith as a good

Christian. Seen in this light, his life story is a wonderful introduction for nonbelievers in psychic phenomena. It is a great contribution in its own right—and too often overlooked.

Men such as Cayce are pathfinders. Once they have accomplished their work, it becomes easier for the rest of us to follow and do the same. Cayce was a rare but not wholly unique individual. His gifts were great and so was his contribution, but if we are to properly appreciate Edgar Cayce and his work, we must seize his example and study it as a key that will unlock our own greater potential and achievement. To elevate him to "untouchable" status and place him in a special category that we cannot attain is to detract seriously from the total value of his life. It deprives humanity of a certain degree of hope. Cayce was in the vanguard of human effort; if we admire his work, we can best demonstrate that admiration by trying to follow in his footsteps and continue his work—or at the very least, pattern our efforts on the *principles* he adhered to.

Indeed, Edgar often mentioned in his readings that others were to follow. Several times he repeated the prediction: "First the few, then the many." As with many of his other predictions, this one is essentially true now. It is one prophecy that his own work greatly helped to fulfill.

One of the greatest values of Edgar's work is that he never involved himself in the trivia that is currently the obsession of so many students of psychic phenomena. Every time he used his psychic talent, he used it to help someone. Conveying useful information was his basic purpose. The practical value of helping people to understand themselves, to cope with their illnesses and problems, and to comprehend the nature of mankind and the mysteries of the universe—this was his concern, rather than guessing the turn of a card or which object might be hidden in a series of envelopes. His example is one that should still be used as a standard for psychic work.

It is worthwhile to stress this fact, as it is overlooked by too many people as they fatuously pursue some isolated series of facts culled from Cayce's readings. And it is missed entirely by those who ignorantly think that they have gone beyond Edgar in their own " scientific" explorations of the psychic—but are really light years behind him. The genuine uses of psychic ability are all marked by a common characteristic—they directly benefit human life, either individually or collectively.

As I was preparing this introduction, Edgar appeared clairvoyantly to me to add a few comments regarding what he wished to have stressed. I include them here as he spoke them to me:

"My old associates on the invisible side of things and I are quite alive and well and very eager to assist those who are responsive and open to our help. All that has been accomplished through me in my life as Edgar Cayce can be continued and extended into new areas. We are quietly involved in doing just that here and there among cooperative minds. But we wish it to be known that the expansion of psychic awareness into many fields is still my continuing work—and indeed, the ongoing interest of many people over here.

"It is foolish to think that only I could ever do the kind of work I did. I have always hoped that my whole life work would be a continuing stimulus for the public to search for other psychics who might continue my work—or to look within themselves and develop their own awareness.

"In making up my biography, please emphasize that I, as a human personality, was a modest and simple person who was as skeptical as anyone about my abilities and the information that came through me. But I found that the information seemed to make sense or was valuable to the people for whom it was intended. In time, many evidential facts came through that helped me accept my own ability. It was very difficult for me, as an orthodox and rather fundamentalist Christian, to accept psychic ability—let alone reincarnation—but in time these ideas seemed more and more reasonable. Of course, now I understand them fully and accept them as matters of fact. I know that psychic events are part of our wonderful universe and that God, in His great wisdom, meant man to extend his knowledge through experience, study, and psychic awareness—so as to comprehend both the nature of God and of mankind.

"I hope that my lifetime will help sensible people everywhere to understand the need for greater awareness. If people read about my life work, I think they will find out something wonderful about themselves—not so much in the way of facts, but as an interesting provocation into the quiet wonders that lie in their own mind. To repeat the oft-quoted phrase, 'The mind is the builder.' And to build properly, we must be wise. Wisdom is the main goal of any form of psychic awareness. Let this be the invocative cry for all students of the psychic process, all psychic researchers, and all readers of books about psychic subjects: wisdom is the goal.

"My own life work is really a matter that extends over thousands of years. I am only one of many who move in and out of incarnation with the intent of helping humanity come to understand more about psychic awareness in its diverse forms and uses. I want to emphasize here that I am not the only one doing this. Nor did the work in this area cease when I passed from the physical.

"There has always been a need for greater wisdom in humanity collectively and in each person individually, whether it be in terms of self understanding or our knowledge about our universe, our careers, the physical world, and so forth. Now, as never before, with many serious problems facing civilization, I hope the appeal and potential of developing psychic awareness will be greater than ever.

"Anyone who might review my life work will be able to see where this sort of awareness and interest can be of immense benefit in many areas today. Promoting this interest is part of what I tried to do in my career as Edgar Cayce. It is what I *am* still trying to do! Please let your readers know this."

In the interview which follows, Edgar explains some of the mechanics of his trance and the psychic readings he did. One of his main partners in that work, a spirit entity named Michael, also appears to make a few comments. The statements they make are a bit pungent at times, but this perhaps is only consistent with Edgar and the body of his readings. As Cayce fans will undoubtedly agree, he never did mince words when the facts were due.

Edgar, of course, appears through the mediumship of my good friend, David Kendrick Johnson. I do most of the interviewing, but am joined at one point by Dave's wife Colene, who sat in on most of these sessions. The interview was conducted in early 1973.

Cayce begins with a lengthy opening statement.

Cayce: Well, good afternoon—if you can call a rainy afternoon a "good afternoon." Of course, Virginia used to be like this much of the time. As a matter of fact, it was somewhat depressing at times.

Before we get into the more formal part of our conversation, I'd like to make some comments about the mediumistic state. David works something like I did, strangely enough. When I was in the physical, I thought of my trance state as a kind of hypnotic state, but of course I now know better. The hypnotic trance and the medium's trance seem very much alike to someone on the outside. They are not the same thing at all, however. The medium's trance goes much deeper. He makes contact with his own inner being and goes on from there.

I'm going to describe for you David's feelings as he is going into trance, because I described it differently when I was doing my work. When I was the medium it felt one way, but now that I'm a spook I have a different perspective. Anyway, I think there's a description in one of the books about me that I would become a spot of light and go through a tunnel: that sort of thing. David seems to pass through a "funny-dizzy" period at first. Then, one of the girls [one of David's feminine spirit controls] usually comes in—Rosie or Martha or someone like that. They do something silly for a few minutes to relax David, until he lets go and moves further up into his inner being. He is still connected to his body by the famous silver cord business, but while he's in trance, he's free to do something like astral travel—but it's not quite that. If he's on the astral at all, it's the upper reaches of the astral.

It's hard for me to explain the differences between hypnosis and a medium's trance, because I would not be on solid ground with the medical part of the description. You see, even I thought that my trance state was a hypnotic one for a number of years; I thought that I needed someone talking in my ear. Because I used that method of getting into a trance, I therefore thought that it was hypnosis. But it was no more hypnosis than the guided format that you use in teaching meditation is hypnosis. The medium's trance begins in the same way that any meditation would begin, but the medium has a kind of "trapdoor" somewhere in his makeup. He can zip up into his inner being and be virtually out of his body while someone is using his head. In a hypnotic trance, there's no contact with the inner being—just the subconscious. And there's no arrangement by which spooks can be entertained.

David works very much as I used to—except that he doesn't like to lie down, for some reason. I did more of a dead trance than David does, though. I was completely out; David sometimes hangs around to listen a little bit. I find it very easy to come through David. I have for a number of years, as you know, because he works very closely to the way I worked.

And there really is no point in turning out lights for a mediumistic trance. Mr. Leadbeater is standing here making some remarks about how he would like to rewrite some passages he wrote on why seances have to be done in the dark. Now he knows better. Actually, the dark seance is a thing of the past. In Mr. Leadbeater's time it was necessary more for the medium's concentration than for anything else.

Incidentally, I should say that I was very mediumistic and only slightly psychic. Most people lump the idea of being psychic together with being mediumistic; they think of them as the same thing. There is a difference. Just because one is a medium doesn't necessarily make him a psychic. In my waking state, I could not begin to do some of the things that you or David can do psychically in your waking states. Both of you are highly psychic as well as being very mediumistic.

Leichtman: I understand.

Cayce: I want to put this on record. During my ordinary waking hours, I was busy maintaining a home and businesses. I never really made much of an attempt to do any kind of psychic work without going into trance. And I am using the label "medium" for myself because it is a word that should be used in the context of my work. None of the material that came from my voice when I was in trance and was so carefully written out, copied, and preserved, was my own thinking. It was that of one of my friends on the invisible side of things.

Well, that ought to suffice for the time being. Maybe we can elaborate on some of these ideas as we go along.

Leichtman: Oh, that will do quite nicely. But would you make some additional comments on a few points? Some of the biographies about you give the impression that most anyone could be placed in a deep hypnotic trance and end up in a state similar to the one you used for all of your work.

Cayce: That would only work in the case of a person who is mediumistic in the first place. And I want to add that being mediumistic is *not* something a person can simply decide to be. It's a rather rare gift. While many people can become psychic, very few psychics can become mediums. It takes the extra "trapdoor."

Leichtman: Is that trapdoor something that one must be *born* with?

Cayce: Yes, but bear in mind that it's something that the mediumistic person usually has earned in some prior lifetime.

Leichtman: So, if he has not been born with that particular gift, he is *not* going to develop it in this particular lifetime?

Cayce: No. Of course, as David says, anyone can call

on his own subconscious to put on a sheet and go "boo," but that isn't authentic mediumship.

Leichtman: Do you mean that the subconscious will respond to one's wishes and mimic mediumship by creating an artificial spirit?

Cayce: Exactly!

Leichtman: Well, then, how does one earn the gift of mediumship?

Cayce: A valuable medium is one who has earned the ability by carefully working in prior lifetimes in this same line. Another one of the ways that people collect the credit points to become mediums is to act as spirit guides on the other side. In a physical lifetime one frequently does not remember doing that, but that is neither here nor there.

In David's case, he has a broad background of experience in several past lives that prepared him for mediumship and created the trapdoor. He has performed a religious function in temples and has studied the body of material which you call "the occult." More to the point, he was a voice that spoke through an oracle at an Atlantean university.

You've had similar experiences which prepared you for mediumship; even Colene [Mrs. Johnson] has the trapdoor, if she would care to use it.

In my case, I had several lifetimes as a medium before I became Edgar Cayce. In fact, I knew David somewhere in ancient Egypt, although I don't think that David has remembered it yet. We worked together as state-sponsored seers.

The interesting thing about my work that you may be fortunate enough to finally get into print is that many of the people who spoke through me identified themselves by name. You have met Michael, who was my major friend in spirit in that lifetime. The being who was known by Arthur Ford as Fletcher also spoke through me, but with a different name. There was a time when even you spoke through me. I am talking about a period of time before you were born as Robert Leichtman.

Leichtman: How about that! Can you comment any further about this group of entities that worked with you?

Cayce: Michael would like to come in after a while and say a few things about that. At times there were twenty to forty beings who would come in and speak. They identified themselves by name, whether it was their actual name or not. I was fortunate to entertain Madame Blavatsky for a short period of time. Much of the material on Atlantis came through her. She did not come through with that name, though—she used another.

Leichtman: Why did she use a pseudonym?

Cayce: Well, at the time I was doing my work it would have been a bit shocking for someone to come in and announce that she was Madame Blavatsky.

Incidentally, now that I have used the name "Michael," someone is bound to read that and decide that it was Saint Michael or the Archangel Michael. Of course, it was neither. It would be very difficult for any medium in a physical body to entertain an angel, much less an archangel. Saint Michael is an archangel: the Archangel Michael, really. They are the same being.

The being named Michael who came through me had been a doctor of sorts, although without portfolio, in central Europe during the period you think of as the Renaissance in Italy. He was really an herbalist doctor. Many of the simpler remedies came from him.

Leichtman: Were there specialists who did health readings and others who did reincarnation readings?

Cayce: Yes, yes. It wasn't quite as departmentalized as that sounds, but there were several health readers and several who did past life work.

I would like to state here that working with past life material is very interesting. I could not get into the Akashic records by myself. The material that came through me was brought by a being who was initiated into the Akashic records and who lived on the invisible side of things. My own inner being could not have gone into the Akashic records. I go into them now, yes, but it's a different situation, as you know.

Generally speaking, physical people do not have direct access to the Akashic records. Of course, they can go into their *own* records—that is, the records of their own past lifetimes. But it's sometimes difficult for them to do even that, depending on how psychic they are.

For the life readings that you do, Doctor, someone else is actually bringing to you material for you to select from. I did not even get complete material; I had to trust the being who selected the material for presentation. Of course, you do more extensive work than I did at that time.

Past life reading is a relatively rare gift. There are maybe twenty people in the United States who can really do it, although there are many more who say they can. I believe there are only four on the West Coast at the moment, in spite of the fact that it looks like thousands. Most of these other people are making something up. I am talking in particular about people who have perhaps four standard plots which they give out to their clients, with only little shadings of difference.

It would be interesting for someone to go through your records or David's—or even mine. It would be seen that no two life readings are the same, and that each reading is helpful to the client. There's always a helpful reason why the client is being made aware of this information—it's not just another pretty story. But when you begin to find a pattern of similar plots in a psychic's file of past life readings, then you begin to realize that perhaps this psychic is behaving in a way that's not quite proper.

I would like to add, too, that there are several games out on the market which purport to help people remember their past lives. They are almost entirely worthless. The people who developed them are really not what they pretend to be. As a matter of fact, the two people I am thinking of at the moment are knowingly fraudulent. They are after the aggrandizement of their bank accounts.

Leichtman: Is there any value in getting information on past lives through the use of hypnotic age regression?

Cayce: Well, the use of age regression into one's *present* lifetime sometimes has a very great value. It's important for people to go back and look at states of mind that they experienced during younger years and take a good look at what was happening. Age regression is a very good technique when used that way. However, hypnosis is a technique that functions in the subconscious almost exclusively, and the subconscious mind is not equipped to handle or entertain the thought of eternity or past lives. As a matter of fact, most people's subconscious minds would sort of shudder at the idea of reincarnation. Of course, as you know, the subconscious is a very willing servant and will manufacture any story you want to hear. But such "recall" is not necessarily a valid past life experience.

In the case of the lady who remembered a great deal under hypnosis about a lifetime as Bridey Murphy in Ireland, that was an accurate lifetime. However, the woman was mediumistic to begin with, and she would have begun to remember some of it anyway, with or without hypnosis.

Leichtman: Is the same thing true of Taylor Caldwell's experiences under hypnosis?

Cayce: This woman is a very fine person and is in a position to do a great deal of good for the cause of psychic and spiritual advancement. But it is blatantly apparent in the book about her past lives that much of it is fantasy rather than actuality. I refer especially to the references to lifetimes on other planets. She got into the fiction department of the astral plane a bit there. It's a pity, because this woman has done so much very fine work. Now she is straining her credibility.

Leichtman: I want to return a moment to a previous subject and ask you more about the large group of spirit entities who worked with you. Did they all belong to some special group? And how did they come to work for you?

Cayce: Well, in the first place, those beings were not my servants, anymore than I am David's servant. Frankly, I come to David and some other mediums because it's an opportunity for me to continue my work. Many of the beings who worked with me did so because it was an opportunity to continue their work—and to make "brownie points" for their own future mediumship, if I may put it that way. This is, of course, a vast oversimplification of how it happens.

A real medium is nothing like the usual variety who purports to give messages from your departed Aunt Minnie. The real medium does quality work; he tries to do something really constructive in the world—such as you are doing with this project. Such a person finds that there are any number of beings who have fine thoughts and are interested in participating in seances. And as the medium progresses, he finds that he attracts more and more spirits who wish to speak. But the people who do the talking don't belong to the medium in any sense of that word. They have simply been invited, in a way, by the medium; the medium's inner being invites them to use the "radio transmitter" of his voicebox and mind.

Fortunately, David has a good enough IQ that he is fairly easy to use for expressing ideas. The intelligence of a medium is very important. Some of the Spiritualists make no effort to develop their minds. They think that being a medium is enough, but that's a very foolish attitude.

Leichtman: Would you comment on how much planning went into your incarnation as Edgar Cayce?

Cayce: Actually, in a broad view, several thousand years. The series of incarnations of any individual on this planet is leading toward an end—not an end in terms of the personality, but an end in terms of the work of the universe. In my case, I had several hundred lifetimes which all worked out in such a way that they led to a rather natural series of life events which permitted me to work as a clear medium. When my efforts are considered in this light, it's a pity that I have been presented to the public as the only person in the world who could do what I did.

There's a spiritual or cosmic law that if one person can do it, then it can be duplicated by others. The groups of people who are interested in studying my work really ought to realize the truth in that more than they do. It's been said that if Jesus could cross the Sea of Galilee without getting His sandals wet, then by the laws of nature, somebody else should be able to do it somehow, too. This is a point that is too often overlooked—or is edited out of the body of material a person might leave behind him.

Leichtman: Did you make much of a point of that spiritual law in your readings?

Cayce [emphatically]: People should remember that I did not do the readings. As a matter of fact, in my ordinary life I was a little bit afraid of going through the body of material that I gave. It was not really a very strong part of my day-to-day life. After all, I had a family to support and many other things to think about. I was very willing to give certain times of the day to this work, but it was not *my* work at that time. I was, after all, something like a radio transmitter, and very little that came out in all that body of material was my own thought.

Leichtman: I see. Since that's the case, was there any effort toward the end of your career to find someone else who could eventually carry on your type of work?

Cayce: Yes. And I believe Michael—or, to be more precise, Michael speaking through my mouth—left a list of names of people who could help carry on the work. I think there were sixteen names on the list. Maybe this would be a good question to ask Michael when he steps in. He spent a good deal of time trying to explain the mechanics of what was going on, and his comments are still in the file that is never presented to the public.

Leichtman: All right, we'll ask him.

Is there anything more that you wanted to say about the preparation immediately prior to your incarnation as Edgar Cayce? Was it definitely planned that you were to be born a medium?

Cayce: Well, certainly. As you know, this is not an accidental universe in any way, shape, or form. There is always a plan, although phrases such as "life plan" or "life mission" are often bandied about by people who don't stop to think about what these expressions mean. They don't understand the full implications of this kind of planning. A series of incarnations for anyone on the physical plane is planned out on a scale that doesn't always relate to the physical personality—if you follow that.

Leichtman: Yes.

Cayce: Generally, the plan is of such a scope that most people would be stunned if they really understood it.

Yes, there was a great deal of planning that went into my becoming Edgar Cayce, just as there was a great deal of planning that went into you becoming Robert Leichtman, or you *[nodding to Colene]* becoming Colene Johnson, or even David becoming David Johnson. But the planning is on a scale that transcends Edgar Cayce, Robert Leichtman, Colene Johnson, and David. It's on a scale that encompasses one's whole being.

May I have one of those? Not one of those, one of these. *[Cayce points to David's cigarets, which were next to another pack on the table.]*

Leichtman: I was going to offer you a cigaret. Would you like a cup of coffee, too?

Cayce: No, a cigaret will be fine. I'm going to be smoking this as much for myself as for Madame Blavatsky [an ironic allusion to Madame Blavatsky's desire for cigarets whenever she appears through David]. As a matter of fact, the good Madame is close by and is also going to partake. I'm not sure I can do this as well as she could. *[Laughter.]*

Oh, while we are diverting ourselves, I would like to depart a little bit and mention David's famous "extra organ" in here. *[Cayce points to David's abdomen.]* You once looked at it clairvoyantly and described it rather nicely, calling it a solidified solar plexus. This is another reason why it's comfortable to come through David. I had one of these, too, but didn't understand its value to mediumship. At one time in my life I thought that I had been smoking too much, and that the smoking had caused this condition.

But I now know that it was an "extra organ" in here. It might not be an organ that could be found on a dissecting table; it's more a peculiarity in the nerves in the solar plexus region. I believe the most profound "extra organ" in modern times belonged to Sophia Williams, the medium and psychic. Is that her correct name?

Leichtman: I think so, yes.

Cayce: Hers was so well organized that the spirit could speak through it. It was almost as if she had two mouths.

Leichtman: Are you referring to the times when she did what is called "independent voice"? [Independent voice is a variety of mediumship in which the "voice" of the spirit emanates from some place other than the medium's mouth.]

Cayce: Yes. Frequently she didn't even hear it. I think you've read about some of the experiments in which a microphone was hung over her solar plexus, and while she read a magazine, the spirits spoke to people in another room! Since her passing she's been accused of being a very clever ventriloquist. But if she did practice ventriloquism, it was only for entertainment at parties—certainly not as a means for convincing anyone that she was conversing with a spirit. In fact, she did not hear much of the conversation that came through her solar plexus and was transmitted over the electric wiring.

Her "extra organ" was unusually well developed. There have been other psychics and mediums in other times who were able to develop it, too, but it is even rarer than the form of mental mediumship that I enjoyed in life and that David enjoys now. I'm using the word "enjoy" in a bit different sense than it is ordinarily taken.

And speaking of enjoyment, H.P. is really enjoying the smoke, too. So, excuse me if I'm being more silent than need be.

I know that there have been a couple of requests for health readings.

Leichtman: Yes.

Cayce: During my life, it was convenient for someone to give the name, age, and whereabouts of the person involved, but that's not necessary now. In the case of the young lady with the eye problem, for example, I can perceive the problem without needing to know her name. It's easier for me now. And please remember that now that I'm working as a spirit, I can do health readings, but in my lifetime I was not doing that work. I want to make that distinction rather clear.

This young lady, who I understand has a problem of blurred vision, is essentially very nervous. The muscles that make up the iris of the eye are responding to this nervousness. In her case, the problem can be very simply handled. She needs to be more careful about using her glasses and more careful about the type of light she uses when she is reading. For the time being, she could take vitamins A and C, or anything that would create a slight acidic condition in her system. When she finds that she can get a little more rest and can get off of her whirlwind of activities, the problem will clear up by itself. She needs to take more care of herself. If she puts ice cubes on her eyelids in the morning and lets them melt while she rests, this will help. That sounds very strange, but the ice cubes will help the iris tone itself up a bit. I suppose oculists all over the United States are going to throw ice cubes at David for letting this advice come through, though. *[Laughter.]* She has admitted drinking, and she has the idea that perhaps the drinking has something to do with her problem. Is that right, Colene?

Colene: She may have said that.

Cayce: Of course, I eavesdrop more than you think I do. *[Laughter.]* The drinking—particularly when she drinks excessively—tends to relax the muscles in the eye, which makes it more difficult to focus them. Her problem here is something like that of the athlete who has to tone up his muscles. For all intents and purposes, it's a problem of the muscles of the iris. I don't think that's medically correct, is it, Doctor?

Leichtman: Well, the iris is a muscular tissue, and in a way it would be accurate to speak of the iris as a "muscle." But the muscle which regulates the focus of the lens of the eye is the ciliary body just behind the iris.

Cayce: She should also use tinted glasses more than she does. She has a glare problem just as David does, and sunlight is helping to weaken the muscles. She needs to be more careful about wearing tinted glasses, particularly when she goes to the beach. She's going to have to sit herself down and do something about her nervousness. She's a very nice young lady, but she's also very highly strung. A creative person often has this kind of problem with nervousness, and sometimes it's very difficult for such a person to live with his or her own makeup. In her case, drinking in moderation would be good for her—particularly beer. It will help her eye problem, too. She may say, "Yeech," when she hears this, but—

Leichtman: For the record, what is the nature of the eye problem?

Cayce: She wears glasses to read with now. They are corrective glasses, and she has also been given corrective exercises. However, it is not really an eye problem; it's a nervous problem. She is not negatively nervous—it's not destroying her as it does some people. She does channel her nervous energy into many things. Really, the problem is more one of overstraining a muscle that is not particularly strong—the iris, that is. Photophobia is not the problem.

She is also using up a great deal more of her visual purple than is ordinary. She knows about this, and the vitamin A would tend to rebuild that. Visual purple problems, incidentally, seem to be rather chronic in the United States.

Leichtman: Not enough carrots? *[Laughter.]*

Cayce: Well, not enough vitamin A. As you know, one would have to eat thousands of carrots to get enough vitamin A. But many of the skin problems that you see in Americans are also due to the fact that they do not consume enough vitamin A.

Leichtman: Let me ask about my eye problem, since I am a high myope. Is there anything that I can do to help myself?

Cayce: Well, you could take a page from David's book and couple your clairvoyant abilities with your actual visual faculties. It's much more simple than it sounds: your inner being has twenty-twenty vision, if you will allow me to put it that way. If you can couple your clairvoyant vision with your physical vision, it will help. It's just a question of shifting your mind around to thinking that way, really. It would greatly improve your eyesight, although you probably always will have to wear glasses, since you've had this particular problem for quite a while.

You could stand more vitamin A, too. And I would recommend capsules rather than carrots, although you like carrots. You also need to get out in the sun more than you do—but weared tinted glasses when you do.

It isn't just the vitamin D from the action of the sun that you need—there are several other things in the radiations of the sun that would be beneficial to you. They would particularly help your eye problem. And as for your problem with your figure, getting out and *walking* on nice days would be beneficial, too. *[Laughter.]*

Leichtman: I don't know about that!

Cayce: It's not fair to hit a spook! *[More laughter.]* But you are at an age in life when getting out and walking for an hour or two in the sunshine would be very beneficial anyway. When a person becomes more interested in being outgoing, his vision tends to become stronger. Part of this is due to occult reasons; you are coupling physical vision with some of your psychic ability. If you do this, you will find that you can see quite well.

Leichtman: Very well.

Cayce: David, incidentally, needs to wear his glasses a little more in the evening than he does. *[He turns to Colene].* Colene, you aren't using your sour cream and honey, are you?

Colene: No.

Cayce: Colene has something that is not really a digestive problem. She has some—well, the phrase "chemical peculiarities" is going to make her sound like a freak, but everybody has metabolic peculiarities.

Leichtman: Do you mean "idiosyncrasies"?

Cayce: Thank you, yes. Sour cream and honey and yeast would, if used once a day at least, keep your little problem under control. Now, this is a medication that is to be used in other ways, too. It can help your cuticle if you massage it in a bit once or twice a day. Doesn't that sound sticky and messy?

Colene: Yes, it does.

Cayce: You do have the right kind of yeast. Be sure that the yeast is dissolved when you are preparing this concoction. And once you've mixed it up, let it sit for a while before you take it.

Colene: If I mix up a larger amount in a blender, it probably will be less lumpy.

Cayce: Yes, and it needs to sit at room temperature for about an hour before you use it—or before you refrigerate the bulk of it.

Colene: Yes. It really doesn't taste bad.

Cayce: Well, you can adjust it and add other things to make it taste better. I'm going to let you have some fun with the recipe that I gave you, Colene; the whole point of letting it stand at room temperature is to let it ferment a bit.

Colene: Oh, I see.

Cayce: Sometime when you are making the batter for sourdough pancakes, you might even try adding some of this mixture to it. A tablespoon twice a day or two tablespoons once a day of this disgusting mess is about what you need.

Colene: Oh, I see. I didn't know how much to take, and I ate a whole dish of it last time.

Cayce: And don't mix up a gallon of it at a time. Also, it's very important that you get real sour cream and not imitation. But you can vary the proportions any way you want, so that it can taste good—well, as good as possible, considering the ingredients.

I'm going to let Michael come in now, as there are some things he wants to talk about. I'll be back in later.

[There followed a pause while Edgar withdrew from David's body and his friend Michael entered.]

Michael: I'm going to say this again. I am *not* Saint Michael! I am *not* the Archangel Michael! I'm just plain Michael. I don't even think I was a historically important person, but I did know an awful lot about herbs and their lore. I don't even know the modern name of the country that I lived in at that time. I traveled around quite a bit; I was something of a vagabond.

You have some questions you want me to answer, I think.

Leichtman: Well, yes, there are several. What's the possibility of anyone carrying on the sort of readings that Edgar did?

Michael: There are a number of excellent people who can do this. I gave a list of names just before Edgar passed over. However, these people are being very seriously hindered by the attitudes of the organization at Virginia Beach [the Association for Research and Enlightenment, which Cayce founded]. They are making a mistake in making a cult out of Edgar, and they have been told so. Edgar and I and some of the other beings have tried to correct the state of affairs there now. But the people we have been able to speak to have always turned a deaf ear, and that's lamentable. I will say this: they have done a lot of very excellent work in bringing this material to the attention of the general public. They have popularized what I'm going to call the "serious trance." That's a much better label than calling it "Edgar's work." There's a danger in personalizing this work too much. And there's danger in thinking that nobody else can do it. That's a shame. The people at Virginia Beach are actually hindering psychics who could continue this work by ignoring them and, in several cases, by not giving them some kind of sanction in the Association, and that's a bad thing. We had hoped that the work would be continued.

I believe that one son is going to be retiring pretty soon, and maybe something will happen in the organization that will bring through some fresh work. Perhaps what little we are saying here today about the situation will be enough to excite some interest in continuing the work—by adding to it.

Leichtman: Yes, I hope so.

Michael: I don't want to sound as though we're bringing a very strong indictment, but we are a little disappointed that no provision was made for us to continue.

Leichtman: I understand.

Michael: I gave some rather specific statements toward the end of Edgar's life about the organization of the Association, and these have been widely overlooked. Part of the problem is that none of the people at Virginia Beach were ready for the fame they are now enjoying. They were very busily running around trying to get things started and did not, unfortunately, get everything done. It's time now that this should be corrected.

Leichtman: Is there more you want to say about the people who can carry on your work?

Michael: The names I gave were of people who, in some cases, were two or three years old at the time. All of the people except one are still living and are quite capable of picking up where Edgar left off.

We wish we could work more through the Association, but as long as that remains difficult, we carry on our work through other channels. In fact, we find it rather easy to slip through David's work and give remedies and other things when necessary. The being known to you as Dr. Kammutt, who comes through David frequently, also spoke through Edgar occasionally. His work is very closely aligned with that of the Akashic readers who came through Edgar. Dr. Kammutt also works with about ten other people who are continuing to do life readings.

I don't want to pin a medal on David particularly, but

neither do I want it thought that nobody else but Edgar can do this.

Leichtman: Edgar mentioned that before I took over this physical incarnation, I was one of the entities who spoke through him. Is that correct?

Michael: Yes. I believe you used one of your favorite "code names" when you came through him. In particular, the material in the readings that dealt with the life of Christ was delivered by you, and some other entities that had been alive during His lifetime.

I might add here that some of the descriptions of the life of Christ [in the readings] were garbled a bit as they came through. I believe that someone else in this project will discuss what happens in this kind of mediumship— that the nature of the medium's conditioning can sometimes create a few distortions in the information presented. The description of Christ's physical appearance in Edgar's readings is somewhat in error and can stand to be corrected. I will have to leave it at this: the artist Rembrandt was shown a vision of the actual appearance of Christ. He made every effort to find a model that came close to that—and then was able to even transcend the model. His paintings are perhaps the closest to the actual appearance of Christ's face that have been put on canvas. I would rather refer you to them than try to give you a verbal description, because Rembrandt's paintings are worth looking up and studying.

In the standard American Christian way of thinking, which I suppose has been somewhat augmented by the Catholic Church, the Christ is pictured as blond, fair, and Nordic. Of course, historically this was not the case. He was rather plain in feature. There was a quality of great beauty about Him that left a very strong impression on people, but it was not due to His physical features.

Leichtman: I understand. I asked Edgar some questions about the large group of spirits who worked through him. Now I have one that I will direct to you: were many of these people members of the White Brotherhood [see glossary] or some other group?

Michael: Many of them are members of the White Brotherhood, but not all of them. Of course, we didn't talk about it: if information of this kind had been made public during Edgar's lifetime, or even when the first books about his work came out, the timing would have been very bad. There was a feeling at that time that the White Brotherhood was something akin to what Madame Blavatsky discussed with you—some kind of an "Elk's Club" in Canada, with men running around in white gowns and somehow being mysteriously helpful. At the time when Edgar was working, it was not appropriate to talk about such ideas at length. Also, Edgar happens to be aligned with another group of beings on the inner planes. It's not necessarily "lower" in importance; it's just another organization.

Leichtman: Well, that's the idea I wanted to bring out: that there are several organizations on the inner planes which are grouped together to perform specific activities that are helpful to the earth plane.

Michael: This particular group (and I'm including myself and Edgar, who was for a time the physical representative of the group) is a sub-group that is specifically working to promote a public awareness of psychic people and psychic events in the physical plane. We intentionally direct our work at stimulating the thinking of the general public concerning psychic awareness.

Leichtman: I presume, then, that this group still maintains this interest and activity?

Michael: Yes. The activity is going forward apace in

spite of limitations that have been put on our activities by the Association for Research and Enlightenment. These limitations are what's so very unfortunate: the people at Virginia Beach have popularized work that was intended to continue, but they don't like the idea of somebody else being able to pick it up.

Leichtman: How would you like to see this work extended? Should it be more of the same, or something in a new area?

Michael: It would have its most profound effect in modern medicine and psychology. There are many doctors and psychiatrists who are becoming interested in this work through the writings that are now so popular in the United States. This popularity is at least opening some doors there for people such as yourself, who can in one way or another continue the work, with or without the official sanction of the Association. It is at least making people ask questions in more scientific areas than would otherwise have happened.

Leichtman: Yes. There seemed to be three categories in Edgar's readings: the health readings, the reincarnation readings, and readings that dealt with general philosophy—although spiritual philosophy certainly permeated both of the other categories, too. Do you see the work that dealt with past lives and philosophy being promoted and extended in new ways, as well as the work that related to medicine?

Michael: Yes. As a matter of fact, we are very excited about extending some of this material into the visual arts. This is a field in which this type of work will have a very important impact. In the hands of gifted and trained artists, the psychic inspiration that came through Edgar as readings can become paintings or pieces of music. Such applications of psychic insights are often far more effective than a dry reading.

Leichtman: Are you talking, then, about training competent artists to develop some type of clairvoyance?

Michael: Artists, especially those who have dedicated a good share of their life to the study of art and are somewhat gifted, are often already clairvoyant—even though they might not use that label to describe themselves. Quite frequently their artwork is psychically inspired. It would be a good thing if there were an outlet or place where such artwork could be shown and discussed. Incidentally, David will be getting himself into a project such as this later on.

There could also be a great deal done by you and some other people in teaching these artists a more controlled use of their clairvoyance. As an example, you have been able to help David make some changes in his painting techniques. If you taught a course for artists, it might not be financially rewarding, but it would be very rewarding in other ways. And in the long run it would be financially rewarding for you, too, although I know you accept money as a secondary part of your work. After all, you are entitled to that, and you should expect to receive material rewards from your gifts. This is why gifts are given to people—so they can make their way in life.

Edgar did not need an income from his readings. He felt it was a very important duty for him to do this particular work. He was quite content about it. There are other people who do not expect income from their work—they do it out of a religious sort of feeling and can continue because their income is from another source. But drawing income from psychic work is not wrong: there's nothing unspiritual about it. People certainly support their ministers without thinking them to be unspiritual for taking the money.

Leichtman: Yes. Are there plans for extending this work into the hard sciences, such as physics and chemistry?

Michael: Yes, there are going to be a number of very startling breakthroughs in the hard sciences—within this decade yet. It's going to become very difficult for even the most skeptical physicist not to appreciate that God is behind everything. There's going to be a movement, even in the hard sciences, back to recognizing a primal source. I don't know how this is going to be accomplished specifically, but it will have to be. It's a little bit cumbersome to work with the mechanism in David's mind and talk about hard sciences. I would have to take some poetic license, which isn't desirable. And I don't particularly want to discuss it today, anyway. *[Laughter.]* Someone else [Nikola Tesla] would like to talk about that subject on another occasion.

Leichtman: To change the topic entirely, would you care to comment about any of the startling predictions that were spoken through Cayce?

Michael: The material as it is seen by the general public is not the same as it is in its original form. The Association for Research and Enlightenment very carefully edits material that goes out of there, including the things they send to their members—for example, the health readings. Unfortunately, the editing process tends to misrepresent some of the material rather seriously, particularly what was said about earth changes. In turn, this information has been exaggerated by the fanatic types of minds who are drawn to write books based on it.

Certainly there are going to be some changes in the world. But if people would pick up the published material—such as the pamphlet called "Earth Changes"—and read it carefully and without emotion (which I know is asking a lot of most people), they will discover that the predictions were not as they have been presented in the rumors. The rumors—particularly about the state of California going off into the ocean—have been so blown up by hysterical people that you would be surprised how tame the material that came through Edgar really is. *Anybody* would.

The government map included in that pamphlet indicates, for example, that the piece of real estate that you are sitting on now here in Carmel [California] is safer than Virginia Beach. This is published, but it's amazing how few people see it.

There are going to be changes, because the planet is evolving. The planet has changed; ever since its creation it has changed. Some of the geological changes have been abrupt, but not nearly as abrupt as rumor would have it.

I want to say something for the record about the people who pass around these rumors. This is something you already know, but it's worth putting in print. These are people with a certain type of mind—a mind that grabs on to the idea that there will be an earthquake in California in such and such a year with great glee, because they find themselves in their own opinion wicked. "Isn't it wonderful that all those wicked people in California are going to get *theirs*—that makes *me* feel better!" That's the sort of "thinking" they use.

I don't know why the rest of the United States wants to think that California is so wicked—any more wicked than any other part of the United States. This is something I have never been able to understand. Maybe it's because there's such an emphasis on recreation out here. Mankind wants to have its recreation, but people have a tendency to think of it as being wicked and frivolous. Thus, they deserve to be punished for it—or some cockeyed notion of that sort. It's the usual doublethink.

Can we leave the earthquakes now? Far too much is said about earthquakes.

Leichtman: All right. I don't have a long list of questions. Why don't you select the topic?

Michael: Well, I'll let Edgar pick the topic—we're going to trade off again. We can do this fairly easily.

Leichtman: Very well.

[A brief pause ensued while Michael was turning over the use of David's body to Edgar.]

Cayce: There is something I would like to talk about: the willingness of groups of people to form little cliques around some psychic adventurer, and the unwillingness of certain psychic types to exchange the knowledge they have acquired with other people a little more freely. There is such a great jealousy among all these people; it's really a sort of crime. I am not talking about the A.R.E., I'm talking about all sorts of groups in the United States. They form themselves around some psychic event or some psychic (and pity the poor psychic who is caught in the middle of all this) and try to keep all of the "true knowledge" to themselves. They do leak little bits and pieces here and there, but in general their attitude is pitiful. I suppose that the need to belong to some kind of an organization is such a strong element in the American consciousness that most people who get interested in occult work want to be part of some so-called occult organization. It makes them feel as though they belong. This attitude stems in part from the fact that America is a new country; as a result, it's going to prevail for a while into the future.

The thing I find really distasteful right now, from my

point of view, is that my personality and work are blown up almost to proportions of a saint. The people—I almost want to say "vultures"—who have descended on my work and have gone over it and over it have not really added anything to it. They have certainly subtracted a great deal one way or another. And it's a pity that the files of my work are not more freely exchanged with other groups.

There is going to have to be more freedom and trust among people and a little less clubbishness if the spiritual age is going to occur. It's a great mistake for someone to set himself up as a head guru and try to establish a clique of insiders around him. I'm thinking of several places in Colorado and California where you have to pay so much a month to get any of their tuition at all. They certainly would not let anyone who is outside of the group look at their files or share any of the information they have gotten. Nor would they recognize that a psychic in another group has any right to exchange an idea with them. This is really childish. It's the sort of thing you see fourth grade students doing. Sometime soon an arrangement must be made to permit the exchange of ideas and information.

Then there are the people who receive these great grants to study psychic phenomena and spend it finding a rather unpleasant person to make pictures on pieces of film. Or they study someone who really is not trained or very talented psychically. The people who do this sort of "research" really don't know very much. Yet they come out with great pronouncements and write volumes and volumes of what amounts to drivel. It's really very distressing and serves no purpose except to continue misconceptions.

I am also distressed that some of the currently popular publications dealing with psychic matters tend to go after articles written by people who really don't know very much and who sensationalize their reporting. It seems that these people who are publishing and pursuing research projects about the psychic don't really look around and see what's going on. I'm distressed by this sort of blindness in people. They report a trivial story in gushing detail, such as: "I had an experience in which my Aunt Tillie came back and rapped on the foot of the bed the day after her funeral." This is fine, you know, but it's not really a contribution to human knowledge.

There is one very slick and professional magazine which is concerned with the subject of psychic phenomena and related fields. Somehow, whenever this magazine comes out, it always reports on the people who are already famous—and who've been saying the same things for years. It seems to just go around in circles.

Leichtman: What would you like to see done? How would you like to see this organized?

Cayce: The public interest in psychic matters is great enough at the moment to support a periodical that is really an open forum. Something like your medical journals would be very healthy. I know, for instance, that you would hesitate to send many of your ideas to some of these magazines because you don't want the onus of publishing them in association with the drivel that would surround them. There's a need for a forum where they would print thoughtful material on a regular schedule, whether or not they paid for it. Something very interesting could grow out of that kind of setup—ideally, a forum that would serve no one's particular interest or pet peeve.

Leichtman: What would you think about a loose organization of psychics that could do professional readings for diverse people and interests, be they personal readings, scientific readings, medical readings, or whatever?

Would this be a good idea?

Cayce: Yes, it could be a very good idea. However, it would be subject to some of the same pitfalls that have historically plagued the so-called artist's colony. Psychics and artists have a number of characteristics in common. I hesitate to say "temperament," because it is much more than that.

Such an organization would need to allow as much freedom as possible for everybody concerned. And it would have to be a group of mature people who are willing to survey what they have done in the past and re-evaluate it periodically themselves—but without the type of pressure that can be brought to bear in another kind of organization. It would also be advantageous if such an organization kept its files open to other members of the profession, although I know it would be difficult to control. A loose organization such as you are describing could do quite well from the standpoint of providing clerical help, which is something no psychic ever has enough of. I was fortunate, but most psychics are so overwhelmed just by the clerical aspect of their work that it is frightening.

Leichtman: What about the work of training psychics, either natural psychics or average people, to develop competent and controlled use of psychic powers?

Cayce: The person who is leading the training has to be psychic and have a very broad use and control of his psychic abilities. The initial training can be very short and to the point. For the budding psychic, there needs to be a controlled period of work, if you follow that. He should work under the direction of someone who has been working in the field for awhile—a kind of apprenticeship, you might say. The training needs to be on a regular basis.

One of the problems in the way you teach now is that

you teach and then go away and don't come back. You do better than some, but the students need to be given a regular series of projects to work on—projects that can be monitored by someone who is experienced in working psychically. The main problem you encounter is that people are a bit lackadaisical about continuing on with the psychic work and experimenting. If they were given definite projects to do together as a group and that sort of thing, it would be better. Of course, I am not suggesting the silly kind of projects that some people come up with, such as attempting a life reading.

I'm getting a bit fuzzy. We're going to pause for just a minute and let David up.

[After a short rest, David went into trance again and the interview resumed.]

Cayce: I'd like to talk on auras for awhile. I suppose I could say that my work is partly responsible for the fact that auras are enjoying popularity right now. But the whole idea of auras has been blown out of proportion.

The word "aura" is usually taken to mean a very easily-seen emanation that surrounds the body right here *[gesturing]* very close—an inch or so away from the actual flesh. Seeing this "aura" is such an easy thing to do; almost anyone can do it. But it doesn't really add to anyone's knowledge.

The *real* aura is a body of energy that is part of your...I was going to say part of your physical body. Of course, it is not: your physical body is part of your aura! The actual aura sometimes extends thirty or forty feet above one's head and ten or twelve feet out from the physical body. There are very few people who can see this kind of aura. One would have to be a very gifted clairvoyant to see it at all.

I suppose the reason why the aura has become so popular is that many people need to be able to work in a mechanical way. They need to be able to pick up a book, run through a color scale, and make snap decisions about other people. I suppose that it's really not very harmful to the others—the standard household variety of aura reader is so ridiculous anyway that very few people would listen to them.

We got into the work of putting together aura charts for people. I'm sorry we didn't have a better artist to work with. The information we could put into the charts was very sketchy. We had hoped that someone would come along and pick up this particular project and do a definitive book on it. I know several books have been written: Butler's is perhaps one of the better ones, but I think Leadbeater touched on it somewhat, too. [See *How To Read the Aura* by W.E. Butler and *Man, Visible and Invisible* by Charles W. Leadbeater.]

There's a type of quasi-medium who will superficially read the book that was put together on my work on the aura, studying the elaborate charts and the symbols in them. Then, when they're in trance, they get "visions" of spooks coming in with elaborate headdresses and other images based on the symbols they saw in the book. They're looking through the limitations of their own ignorance when they do this.

Aura reading is perhaps the easiest psychic thing in the world to do. It's something I could even do myself, without being in trance. But the auras didn't tell me very much. Very quickly I learned that every living being has one, and it ceased to be a curiosity for me. I had other matters to put my mind on. I will tell you this: in my work in photography, I did notice that auras "photograph"; it's possible to see an aura on a photograph as well as around a person.

Unfortunately, aura reading is something that can be used to damage another person. You know, the usual thing: a person will tell you, "You've got a purple aura, which means you must have had bad past incarnations." And then he'll insist that you do so and so to compensate—whatever made-up penalty he has connected with purple. But it's really impossible to do a reading of that sort based on the colors in the standard flesh-clinging aura. People are deluding themselves and others when they try to do it.

I certainly don't think that the games and printed material about auras that have come out have anything to do with my work. There are people who use their perception of auras to put together *objets d'art* that are very nice. They deserve more attention. The whole field of psychic art, if you can call it that, is going to be coming more to the fore in the future.

A Scientologist gentleman recently published a rather unfortunate article on what he called "cosmic art." But the people described in that article are just collecting things that were done in the Aleister Crowley circle. Publicizing that as cosmic or psychic art is a bit unfortunate. This type of "artwork" is generally marked by some kind of geometric, circular pattern. There's no high artistic inspiration to it, and certainly no psychic inspiration at all. At least it's a step in the direction of talking about art, but it's sad that so many of the people who do "psychic art" are just the rankest of amateurs. I would like to see more serious artists take it up.

Leichtman: What type of things should be in an aura chart? What is one really trying to accomplish in creating one?

Cayce: There is some truth in the idea that one picture

is worth a thousand words. Certainly one picture can communicate a great deal to the subconscious mind, because images are the language of the subconscious. Hopefully, an aura chart should convey some kind of a healing or beneficial effect, whether it was understood or not, and not just be a painting that gives one a wild, artificial thrill. And there's also something to be said for the aura chart being a pleasant picture to look at. It doesn't necessarily have to look as spooky as some of them currently do.

Leichtman: How does one pick out which symbols, colors, or pictures should be put in the aura chart?

Cayce: It takes a trained, skilled artist to do this sort of work.

Leichtman: Who is also a psychic?

Cayce: Who is also a psychic, yes. It should be a trained, dedicated artist who is very much interested in the healing aspect of his art. Such an artist would be able to intuitively pick up from someone's aura symbols and colors of a healing, beneficial nature.

Leichtman: Are these symbols or colors literally seen in the flesh-clinging aura?

Cayce: No, they are not literally seen. An artist can take an abstraction and make a drawing out of it. Depending on the artist, of course, the actual impression would come in one of several ways.

David is one artist who is working with auras. And there are several others who put together aura charts that may look a bit like surrealistic paintings, but they are not uncomfortable or unpleasant. As a matter of fact, they are works of art that a person can hang up and look at and feel comfortable with. And in time, the deeper meanings in these paintings start communicating with the subconscious mind.

Leichtman: I see. Are you implying, then, that the artist does not just see colored lights in the aura but perceives the quality of someone's consciousness and then translates it into a symbolic picture?

Cayce: I really don't think I could say it better myself. *[Laughter.]* That's what I was driving at, yes. It's very much like the way that psychics perceive spooks, if you will. We actually appear rather like a ball of light or energy, but there's a translating mechanism in the psychic or medium's head that puts arms and legs and heads and clothing on the image. Of course, we stimulate this kind of impression when we make contact with the psychic or medium, because it's easier to deal with a spook that looks somewhat human. It's also easier for the psychic to maintain contact if the spook keeps more or less in the character of one of his or her physical incarnations.

You're about to burst with a question, aren't you?

Leichtman: Yes. I want to inquire if it is necessary for a psychic to see colored lights around a person in order to "read" his aura or analyze its significance?

Cayce: Oh, no—he does not have to see anything. The parts of the aura that get read most commonly—for example, the colored lights—really don't tell you very much. It's the intuitive interpretation that a psychic picks up that is really important.

Leichtman: What aspect of this energy field or aura is being photographed in Kirlian photography?

Cayce: Kirlian photography at present mainly picks up the etheric part of the aura—and will be limited to that until it is studied and played with a bit further. The etheric is the high physical plane, as you call it. It's not really terribly much of the aura; it's the little skin-clinging aura that most people see.

Leichtman: Is that sometimes called the "health aura"?

Cayce: It can be, but that's an American shortcut word. You know, Americans—and I was very pleased to be one myself—Americans have a tendency to want to have short-cuts for everything.

To finish my idea on Kirlian cameras, it's a good thing that many people are experimenting with this type of photography; eventually it will be seen that the Kirlian camera can also pick up part of the astral body. Of course, that will require a much more complicated camera. Someone mentioned in one of these interviews that it will eventually be possible to map the subconscious mind, and I believe it's going to be done with a complicated Kirlian camera.

Leichtman: Very good. While we are on this subject, is it possible by conscious effort to radically alter the astral aura? Can someone attempt to fool another person by doing this deliberately and deceptively?

Cayce: That's very easily done—beginning metaphysicians can do it. Of course, someone who is chronically uncomfortable with reality can also do it. After all, the astral plane is a place of great fantasies; certainly one can surround himself in fantasy.

Leichtman: So, if someone is seen with a nice, lovely pink aura, he may not really be happy and polite and gentle?

Cayce: Of course. If all a person can read is the astral aura, he's in trouble—because it's often misleading. He must also read the mental aura, if I may put it that way. It's very difficult to deceive someone with the mental aura—no matter what "sugarcoating" might be in the astral aura. The elements in the mental aura are not seen as colors and lights—you know this yourself. They are "seen" more as realizations about a person's character. You can do this quite easily, and have had many sudden insights about people that have proven quite accurate. You do good work at times.

Leichtman [laughing]: Thank you. Can I change the subject?

Cayce: Of course.

Leichtman: Many times the health readings gave advice or remedies to individuals with specific diseases. How well can those remedies be applied to other people with similar illnesses?

Cayce: This is something I wish someone could do a research project on. Unfortunately, in the structure of the A.R.E. now, it's nearly impossible to do. Even the group of doctors that is working with this material has not gone into it extensively. Some of the readings were given for an individual cure. Bear in mind that each human being is a complete system and is slightly different than any other human being. All cures aren't going to work on every human being.

We made this point to David some years ago. A gentleman wrote to him and wanted to know if he could contact either me or the readers [the spirits, such as Michael, who worked through Edgar]. He asked if the very gooey remedy for baldness would work on him. It does work on some people.

Leichtman: You're referring to the use of crude petroleum on the scalp?

Cayce: Yes. *[Chuckling.]* I remember that when I read the notes of the sitting in which that cure was first described, I thought: "What a mess!" I wouldn't use it myself, but for the particular person it was originally given to, it did work. It will cure a certain type of baldness, but it's not a very common type. It's designed to stimulate what some barbers now call a "growth pad"—here. *[Cayce pointed to the back of David's head.]* Sometimes it's the only way the growth pad can be stimulated.

The olive oil treatment that you used would work more generally. Actually, one of the best ways to prevent baldness is proper washing and rinsing of the hair, which most men never learn how to do. It has to be started in youth, though; it can't be taken up at the age of thirty in the expectation of growing more hair.

Leichtman: I understand.

Cayce: There are many times when these remedies might be used that they would have no effect whatsoever on a condition. For instance, the advice I gave Colene has been designed especially for her. If another woman had her exact condition, then it could also work on her, but it would not work on every woman.

Leichtman: How should the medical profession use your body of records for medical treatments of current illnesses?

Cayce: One intelligent thing they could do is contact a medium that I could talk through. That would make a great deal of sense, but of course it doesn't seem to be occurring.

Leichtman [in mock protest]: But Edgar, the rumor is that you *never* appear through a medium!

Cayce: Fancy!

Leichtman: I'm sorry.

Cayce: Another way would be to conduct a series of controlled experiments on this material.

Leichtman: Yes, I think this is being done now, in part.

Cayce: The time is coming soon when some of these suggestions are going to be researched very, very carefully and very thoroughly. You're seeing this research growing now, and you chafe at the slowness and—I'll say it—the stupidity of the researchers. But it *is* a beginning. Things are going to be moving very quickly. You know, there *are* intelligent doctors. They don't often get up at psychic meetings and talk, but there are intelligent doctors and scientists that will take up this information and work with it. There are many who are doing it now, but they are not "confessing" to it, because they don't want to be numbered among the silly—the silly, of course, being most of the ones who do get up on the platforms and speak now.

Leichtman: Suppose a group of doctors or other people wished to find a good medium through which you or the other entities who worked with you could speak. How would they know they had found the right medium?

Cayce: There's an old, old statement in the Bible. It's very simply put: "By their acts ye shall know them." Frankly, I can't improve much on that advice; it's the best guide you can have in finding the right medium. You should experimentally listen to various mediums who claim that they can contact me, and base your judgments on the quality of what they say. Unfortunately, too many people go to a medium and accept at face value everything the medium says. They never put anything to the test. Even many "scientists" do this, and it's almost as silly as when housewives do it. As a matter of fact, it's more tragic.

Doctors who are interested in working with psychic material should carefully observe with an open mind anyone who is doing medical readings of any sort. If he can perform, then perhaps he should be listened to.

I am *not* saying that a group of doctors—even the group sponsored by the A.R.E.—should look only for me. There are other people who can do the same work. If the doctors make a little effort to look for some of them, a lot of medical problems could be straightened out very quickly.

Leichtman: Are there thousands and thousands of such mediums?

Cayce: No, there aren't that many. The mediumistic person is relatively uncommon in humanity. Psychic ability is rather widespread, but genuine mediumship is something else again. There aren't thousands and thousands, but there are enough. When the world comes around to a greater understanding of mediumship—for example, the differences in quality between one medium and another—then it will be seen that there are more real mediums around than has perhaps been thought. But they don't number even in the ten thousands. It's a much smaller number.

As we discussed earlier, psychics need to band together. Such groups should also include mediums. That would give them a wider stage, and they could be more objectively observed than is now possible. But of course, the doctors and scientists have to be willing to look for high-quality mediums as well. I don't know why scientists keep running to the low-level people for demonstrations of psychic and mediumistic abilities. They seem to have a knack for finding the worst ones available.

I certainly don't mean to insult someone like Mrs. Garrett [Eileen Garrett, who participated in this project and who was used in a number of scientific experiments while alive] or Mrs. Leonard [Gladys Osborne Leonard, a British medium who was consulted frequently by Sir Oliver Lodge for scientific work]. These women were very fine mediums, and they were very fortunate that the scientists who found them and worked with them were able to help them find the proper stage for their gifts.

You chafe sometimes because you don't receive proper attention. Bear in mind that when I came along I was called horrible names and was held in great suspicion by many,

many people. I did not really ever enjoy a proper stage for my activities. I'm not talking about personal fame now—I'm talking about having an area of activity where I could have been more useful than I was. Fortunately, my work became useful after my passing. I don't think you're going to have to worry about that particularly.

Leichtman: All right. Unless you have something more to say on that, I'll change the subject.

Cayce: I'd like to make a personal suggestion. If you and David would put together a loose "gestalt" group for psychic readings, you could offer a valuable package. Whenever someone applied for a reading, you could do part of it, David another part, and someone else yet another. All of this work would be done independently, however, without anyone being aware of the work being done by the others. Several salubrious psychics working on the same reading could produce something really valuable.

Leichtman: I understand. Michael talked some about using psychic ability as a source of income. Would you add some comments of your own? Just what sort of laws are involved?

Cayce: Anyone who has a gift given to the personality, whether it's a psychic gift or an artistic gift, should understand that it was given to help him make his way in the world. Any psychic or medium who puts service first and then accepts a reasonable fee for the amount of time and effort put into the work is certainly within his rights. There is no karmic problem involved in this: exchange is, after all, one of the laws of karma. Jesus certainly received food, clothing, and shelter for His work. This was reasonable and was expected. It was freely given and accepted.

People who try to make exorbitant fortunes on a little bit of psychic ability are really asking for trouble, though.

Getting paid for your services isn't wrong, but putting the payment before the service *is*. You know one or two psychics who are losing their gifts, not because they are accepting money for readings, but because to get the money they are flattering people and telling them what amounts to lies.

Lying in any way, shape, or form—even if it's a lie of omission—has a very serious karmic consequence. It's something that's not easily balanced. If a doctor malpractices, that produces social karma that has to be taken care of—probably through an expensive court case. When psychics malpractice by being untruthful, society generally takes care of them, too.

The worst kind of psychic, and I think you would agree with me, is the one who runs around being curious about other people's sex life. This is a kind of clairvoyeurism which dwells on the sexual nature or the sexual problems at hand. An example of this is the woman out here who misuses astrology to break up marriages. She has certainly opened a can of worms for herself that she doesn't see yet. She will live to regret it in this incarnation, and will have to atone for it in a couple more incarnations to come.

Another bad problem of this sort is the so-called "psychic group," where a medium encourages a group to come and sit every Thursday afternoon to ooh and aah at every golden pearl that comes from his mouth—for a fee. Of course, the medium is more interested in the money and the prestige than in helping the people who come. This kind of person is not only making serious karmic problems for himself but also for everybody who comes, because the whole thing is based on a desire for status. I think you've seen one or two of these groups in operation. Frequently, the psychic or medium who leads this type of group is not really genuine.

A psychic who does his work and gives his service, and who is then able in his free time to go do something else, is a healthy psychic or medium. Such psychics tend to be much more reliable than people who want to have grand organizations around them and large sums of money in the bank. A psychic or medium needs to put service first: then, the material needs of life will take care of themselves.

Leichtman: What about the use of psychic ability for gambling and for selecting investments?

Cayce: Occasionally, in the materialistic world today, a good psychic will give advice in this area that turns out to be accurate. It's probably a demonstration to show someone the scope of psychic abilities. That kind of thing is sometimes needed. But this kind of advice shouldn't be the primary concern of a psychic. Business readings are certainly within the proper realm of psychic work, but when the psychic is getting an outlandish sum of money for his consultation, then I would wonder about it.

Leichtman: What about advice for outright gambling?

Cayce: I see no reason for giving it, frankly: it's like telling an alcoholic what kind of alcohol to drink, really, or a drug addict what kind of drugs to use for a better high. It would make about as much sense. I know people come to David as they used to come to me—to ask for this kind of advice. I would take the request and file it over here in the wastebasket very quickly. I'm glad to see that David does the same thing. He's going to present Colene's mother with some numbers to play in Reno, but it's because Colene's mother needs an evidential demonstration. She is not a gambler.

In a case where an honest person needs money in a hurry for a good reason (and you have certainly experimented with this yourself), then the advice might be proper. It depends a great deal on the person seeking the advice. If there's an honest need, then perhaps the information can come.

Leichtman: In some of your comments today, you have implied that psychic abilities can be removed if they are not properly used. If they are removed, how are they removed, and is it permanent?

Cayce: And also implied in that is: who does the removing?

Leichtman: Yes.

Cayce: The psychic's own inner being does the removing. Bear in mind that your own inner being is really the "recording angel" you have to worry about. Sometimes psychic ability needs to be removed temporarily, so that the personality of the psychic recognizes his mistakes. This need not be permanent if it's truly recognized—the judge being, of course, the inner being.

There are those personalities (I'm sure you've run into them) who have very seriously misused what little psychic ability they had, and it was quickly removed. However, that didn't stop their careers as "psychics"!

Of course, there are times when even a psychic whose ability has been pretty well removed can still be used to channel bits of information that need to come through—but essentially the ability is gone.

You've been noticing that there has been a cleanup of psychic abuses in the world this last year. There will be less and less of these problems as time goes on, not so much because there will be fewer cheap mediums, but because there are just going to be more and more obviously intelligent ones! Many, many people are mediumistic and know it, but they don't make a public display of their talents because they don't want to be considered "Madame

Zenobias." Well, the time of the world now is such that some of these people will be able to step forward and offer their services—without jeopardizing their business, families, or reputations.

Leichtman: I'm reading my list to see what else I wanted to ask you. I have the topic of astronomy.

Cayce: Do you mean astronomy or astrology?

Leichtman: Astrology, yes. I'm sorry.

Cayce: There's a good deal of material on astrology that hasn't been channeled through mediums or psychics yet. Certainly a great deal was given to Alice Bailey, and I was able to bring through a little. Some distortions occurred, however, because neither Alice Bailey nor I were astrologers or knew anything about that particular art. It would be best for this material to come through someone who is a trained astrologer—but unfortunately, many astrologers prefer to stick to what they call the "scientific routine." This does not allow for inspiration to come through. However, there are growing numbers of inspirational astrologers who are bringing the needed information through. What little I did bring through—as well as the material of Alice Bailey— is certainly going to be very helpful.

The science of astrology will become much more scientific and respectable in the very near future. Getting it straightened out is going to require a rather large research organization with modern machinery. At the moment, it's a project that is too vast for any one astrologer to handle.

As the new astrology emerges, it's going to be so utterly useful that it will be regarded almost in the same light as psychology. That's how it should be regarded, anyway.

Leichtman: What is this new astrology?

Cayce: As it is currently formulated, astrology contains

many mathematical errors—well, they're not exactly errors, but the accurate material just isn't available to the ordinary astrologer. The mathematical material that's available to the dedicated astrologer who wants to do a good job just isn't very good. It needs to be revised. Some of the data coming out of Germany is much more accurate than the American writings and tables. Even so, a great deal of revision needs to be made.

Please bear in mind that I'm not an astrologer, even now. I'm having to ask for advice on the inner planes in order to give you these answers.

You've been talking to David about the case for what is currently called "sidereal astrology," which takes into account the fact that not all of the signs of the zodiac are thirty degrees long. You've also wondered about the merits of what is called "heliocentric astrology." Some of the theories of astrology are going to have to be slightly altered. Astrology will still have to be a geocentric art, because it's dealing with events on the Earth. But as anyone who's gone through grade school knows, Earth is not the center of the solar system. Therefore, for the purposes of charting, the Earth should be taken as a point, rather than a literal center of things. There does need to be a new system of charting; interest in moving in this direction is growing right now.

There also needs to be an improved system of mathematics. Someone needs to go through all the literature and clean up what is called the "delineation"—and what it means. In this particular area, the intuitive astrologer will be in much better shape than the scientific astrologer.

Leichtman: Are you implying, then, that the psychic astrologer will actually be able to redefine delineations?

Cayce: A psychic astrologer can look at even the incomplete charts he's currently restricted to and somehow compensate for what's missing when he gives the delineation of his clients. I would rather use the term "esoteric" astrologer than "psychic," although they mean just about the same thing. A good astrologer can reap reams and reams of information out of any given chart. Of course, he's limited by the amount of time he can spend with any one client, but when it's necessary, a good esoteric astrologer can obtain a great deal of information about the nature of his client from that person's inner being.

I use the word "client" because it is more graceful than "querist." [Laughter.] I don't mean "client" in the sense of someone who pays money necessarily. I don't want to put that coloring on the word. "Subject" may be a better word. "Victim," sometimes. [More laughter.]

Astrology is a tool that can greatly enhance some forms of psychiatric treatment, because not only can an enlightened person read a horoscope, but he can also use the horoscope as a species of sympathetic magic, so that it has a healing effect. I don't want to go into detail on that at all—it's a technique that could also be used to maim and kill, as well as heal. I can't explain it, because I won't be given the information.

Would it be agreeable to call a halt to the proceedings for today? Do you have enough material?

Leichtman: I think so.

Cayce: Well, my dears, thank you very much.

Leichtman: Thank you.

GLOSSARY

AKASHIC RECORDS: The cosmic record of events. On an individual basis, the akashic is similar to the "memory" of the soul and therefore includes a record of all its experiences, both in and out of incarnation.

ANCIENT WISDOM: The knowledge of the soul; a body of teachings which is preserved at the level of the soul and is taught by those advanced individuals who enjoy full contact with the soul.

ASTRAL BODY: Any body or vehicle of life made of astral matter and existing on the astral plane. For humans, the term is the same as "body of emotions."

ASTRAL PLANE: The plane of the emotions and desires. The astral plane is an inner world made of matter that is more subtle than physical substance, yet interpenetrates all physical substance. It is teeming with life of its own. The phenomena of the astral plane differ from physical phenomena in that they occur fourth dimensionally.

ASTRAL TRAVEL: Any form of movement of an entity on the astral plane. The uninformed sometimes use the term "soul travel" to describe this phenomenon, but this is incorrect: the soul pervades everything; it does not travel.

ASTROLOGY: The science of the interplay of cosmic energies. Astronomy is the science of the interrelationship of physical bodies and energies in the universe; astrology is the science of the interrelationship of *all* bodies and energies in the cosmos—astral, mental, and divine ones, as well as physical.

ATLANTEAN: A long stage in human development and civilization which ended catastrophically, through the misuse of its technological achievements. While the focus of growth for the average Atlantean was the nurturing and expression of the emotions, the science of that time reached heights not yet attained in our modern civilization. The period is called "Atlantean" because it was primarily centered on a now-submerged continent in the Atlantic Ocean and was referred to by this name by Plato. The heyday of Atlantean culture lasted from 100,000 to 12,000 B.C.

AURA: The light observed by clairvoyants around all life forms. It emanates from the surface and interior of the etheric, astral, and mental bodies. Clairvoyant observation of the aura can reveal the quality of health or consciousness.

CLAIRAUDIENCE: The capacity to hear nonphysical sounds.

CLAIRVOYANCE: The capacity to see or know beyond the limits of the physical senses. There are many degrees of clairvoyance, allowing the clairvoyant to comprehend forces, beings, and objects of the inner worlds normally invisible to the average person.

DISCARNATE: A human being without a physical body, living on the inner planes.

DIVINATION: The act of discerning the divine order of events and forces in the universe.

ESOTERIC: An adjective which refers to knowledge of the inner worlds and inner life. In this book, it is used to refer to the knowledge of spirit—and to the body of teachings known as the Ancient Wisdom.

ETHERIC MATTER: The substance or "stuff" of the etheric plane.

ETHERIC PLANE: The most subtle realm of the

physical plane. It is composed of the finest grades of physical matter, exceeding even the "fineness" of gases. In physics, the term "plasma" would be used for this grade of matter.

GOD: The Creator of all that exists, visible and invisible; the life principle and creative intelligence underlying all life forms and phenomena.

HEAVEN: The state of consciousness of the spirit. Heaven is not a place populated by those who have died; it is accessible to incarnate and discarnate humans alike. It is a state of mind. In heaven are located the archetypal patterns of all creation, as well as the ideal qualities of human expression.

HIGHER SELF: The animating principle in human consciousness—the inner being or soul. It is the guiding intelligence of the personality, the part of the human mind that is immortal.

HOROSCOPE: A chart depicting the interrelationship and relative strength of astrological forces at the time of birth for an individual, group, or nation. Used wisely, a horoscope can lead to a greater understanding of how cosmic forces influence creative manifestation.

HYPNOSIS: A psychological technique for communicating more directly (and sometimes more forcefully) with the subconscious of an individual. It is an artificial technique that does not make contact with the inner self of the individual.

INCARNATION: The period of time in which a human spirit is expressing itself through a personality.

INNER PLANES: A term used to refer to any one of several inner worlds or levels of existence, all of which interpenetrate the dense physical plane. Each physical human being exists on these inner planes as well as on the physical level, by dint of having bodies composed of matter drawn from them.

INNER SELF: The essence of the human consciousness which is the guiding intelligence of the personality. It is associated with the immortal aspect of the human mind.

INTUITION: In general usage, the capacity to know something without using the physical senses.

INVISIBLE: A discarnate entity.

KARMA: A Sanskrit word meaning "reactiveness." Every one of our actions, thoughts, and emotions produces a reaction of like quality, sooner or later. Good deeds and thoughts produce beneficent reactions; cruel and selfish deeds and thoughts produce restrictive reactions. By dealing with these karmic effects, we gradually learn the lessons of maturity.

KIRLIAN PHOTOGRAPHY: A special type of photography which simulates etheric auras around objects.

MADAME ZENOBIA: A personal term used to describe the type of emotional and unintelligent person whose lust for psychic experience and attention far exceeds their competence or honesty. Their appearance is often notable because of the excess of makeup, jewelry, and oddness of clothing. Despite the obvious handicap, they presume great psychic talent and hold forth as "gifted" clairvoyants and fortune tellers for profit and fame.

MANTIC DEVICE: A set of symbols that can be used for the divination of destiny, duty, and purpose. Numerology, palmistry, the Tarot, and the I Ching are all mantic devices.

MASTER: An individual who has reached complete competence and perfection as a human. The epitome of genius.

MATTER: The substance of life—energy in manifestation. There is mental and astral matter as well as physical.

MATERIALISM: The belief that the physical plane is the only plane of existence, or at least the most powerful and important. Materialism denies the importance of the soul, the existence of divine intelligence, and the invisible realms of life.

MEDITATION: An act of mental rapport in which the ideals, purposes, and intents of the inner life are discerned, interpreted, and applied by the personality. To be meaningful, meditation must be a very active state in which creative ideas, new realizations, and healing forces are discovered, harnessed, and applied to the needs of daily life. The current belief that meditation is a passive state of emptying the mind, by just sitting, is the antithesis of true meditation.

MEDIUM: A person who practices mediumship.

MEDIUMSHIP: The phenomenon of a nonphysical intelligence, usually a discarnate human, assuming some degree of control of a physical body in order to communicate something useful and meaningful. Mediumship is usually used for the transmission of information or inspired guidance, but can also be used to transmit varieties of healing energies. There are varying degrees of trance associated with mediumship and differing qualities of information communicated, depending on the quality of the medium and the quality of the spirit using the process. Mediumship is distinguished from the phenomenon of possession in that it occurs only with the deliberate cooperation of the medium and produces a constructive result.

MENTAL BODY: A separate body or vehicle of intelligence possessed by every human and interpenetrating the dense physical body. In essence, it is the mind (which must not be confused with the physical brain). The mental body is composed of the finer grades of matter drawn from the mental plane. It is the body used for intellectual discernment, analysis and logical thinking. It is different than the astral body, which is concerned with expressing sentiment, emotions, likes and dislikes, and reactions.

MENTAL PLANE: The dimension of intellectual thought. One of the inner planes of existence, it also interpenetrates the dense physical plane. It teems with active life of its own, in addition to providing the substances for the mental bodies of all humanity.

METAPHYSICS: The philosophical and intellectual inquiry into the spiritual nature of all things.

MIND: The portion of the human personality that has the capacity to think. The mind is an organized field of energy which exists in invisible dimensions. It is *not* the physical brain, although it can operate through the brain.

NINE UNKNOWN: A small group of physical people who, in effect, own the planet. They secretly oversee major events of civilization and protect occult knowledge. The label comes from a novel by Talbot Mundy, *The Nine Unknown.*

OCCULT: The hidden secrets of nature.

ORACLE: A divine announcement or prophecy. The place where such a message is received, or the medium or psychic through which it comes, may also be called an oracle.

PERSONALITY: The part of the human being that is used for manifestation in the earth plane. Composed of a mind, a set of emotions, and a physical body, it is the child of the soul and its experiences on earth.

PLANE: An octave in consciousness. All planes of consciousness interpenetrate the same space; they differ from one another in the quality of their substance. The human personality exists in the physical, astral, and mental planes.

PSYCHIC: A person who is able to perceive events and

information without the use of the physical senses. The word is also used to refer to any event associated with the phenomena of parapsychology.

REINCARNATION: The process of the soul evolving through a successive and progressive series of different physical personalities.

SILVER CORD: The symbolic connection between the soul and the physical body. Once the silver cord is snapped, physical death ensues.

SITTING: A seance.

SOUL: The individualized principle of consciousness and creativity within the human being. It is the soul that evolves and acts; it is the soul that creates the potential of the personality, vivifies it, and guides it through certain life experiences designed to increase competence in living. The soul is a pure expression of love, wisdom, and courage.

SPIRIT: In this book, a word used primarily to describe the portion of the human being which survives death. It is this "spirit" that a medium contacts. In this sense, a spirit would be as individualistic as his or her personality was during physical life, retaining both good and bad characteristics. The word is also used to refer to the highest immortal, divine essence within the human being.

SPIRIT CONTROL: A special type of discarnate human who works with a medium. The function of the spirit control is to guard the "doorway" to the medium's mind, to act as master of ceremonies for other spirits who might appear through the medium, and to care for the condition of the medium's body before and during the medium's trance period.

SPIRITUALISM: A religious movement that incorporates mediumship as a central feature of its worship.

SPOOK: An affectionate term for a discarnate.

SYMBOL: An image, thought, or event which contains a deeper significance than what is obvious from the outer form. It points to inner dimensions of reality, force, and meaning.

TELEPATHY: Direct mind-to-mind communication. Most often, telepathy occurs on the astral plane.

TRANCE: A state in which ordinary consciousness is quieted so that another element of consciousness can use the physical voicebox and body.

WHITE BROTHERHOOD: One of a number of select groups whose members are dedicated to the advancement of human evolution and the fulfillment of cosmic plans. It is composed of both incarnate and discarnate people, but functions on the inner planes.

FROM HEAVEN TO EARTH

Edgar Cayce Returns is a single interview in a set of 24 conducted by Robert R. Leichtman, M.D. The full set of 24 are published by Ariel Press in a six-book series called *From Heaven to Earth*. Each book contains four interviews between Dr. Leichtman and the spirits of prominent psychics, geniuses, and leaders. They may be purchased individually for $11.95 per book (plus $2 shipping) or as a complete set for $60, postpaid. The six books in the series are:

The Psychic Perspective—Edgar Cayce, Eileen Garrett, Arthur Ford, and Stewart White.

The Inner Side of Life—C.W. Leadbeater, H.P. Blavatsky, Cheiro, and Carl Jung (with Sigmund Freud).

The Hidden Side of Science—Nikola Tesla, Luther Burbank, Sir Oliver Lodge, and Albert Einstein.

The Priests of God—Albert Schweitzer, Paramahansa Yogananda, Andrew Carnegie, and Sir Winston Churchill.

The Dynamics of Creativity—William Shakespeare, Mark Twain, Rembrandt, and Richard Wagner.

The Destiny of America—Thomas Jefferson, Benjamin Franklin, Abraham Lincoln, and a joint interview with 7 spirits from American history—Hamilton, Franklin, Jefferson, the two Roosevelts, Truman, and Washington.

Extra copies of *Edgar Cayce Returns* are available for $7.95 plus $2 postage.

Orders can be placed by sending a check for the proper amount to Ariel Press, 4255 Trotters Way, #13-A, Alpharetta, GA 30004, or calling toll free 1-800-336-7769. Make checks payable to Ariel Press. Foreign checks should be payable in U.S. funds. Orders may also be charged to MasterCard, VISA, Discover, American Express, or Diners.